MW00789051

I Am!

Love, Wisdom, and Guidance through Soul Reflection

COMPILED BY

NICOLE EASTMAN, D.O.

CM Publisher
c/o Marketing for Coach, Ltd
Second Floor
6th London Street
W2 1HR London (UK)

www.cm-publisher.com
info@cm-publisher.com

ISBN: 978-0-9928173-3-6

Published in UK, Europe, US and Canada

Book Cover and Inside Layout: Alvaro+Livia Beleza

Table of Contents

Foreword 9

Appreciation and Gratitude 11

Introduction 13

CHAPTER 1   **I Am Beautiful**
            By Nicole Eastman, D.O. 16

CHAPTER 2   **I Am Hope**
            By Anthony J. Soave 22

CHAPTER 3   **I Am Fearless**
            By Bernard J. Rabine. 28

CHAPTER 4   **I Am Authentic**
            By Vicki Savini 34

CHAPTER 5   **I Am Free**
            By BrieAnna P. Daugherty, LLPC NCC MA IMH II 40

CHAPTER 6   **I Am Love**
            By Emily Obukowicz. 46

CHAPTER 7   **I Am Grateful**
            By Judith LeBlanc 52

CHAPTER 8   **I Am Present**
            By Kimle Nailer, BA 59

CHAPTER 9   **I Am Valuable**
            By Para-Chaplain Michelle Smith. 64

CHAPTER 10 **I Am Worthy**
            By Samantha Smith. 70

CHAPTER 11 **I Am Wanted**
By Shannon Monticciolo-Davis *76*

CHAPTER 12 **I Am Heard**
By Sheilah M. Wilson, M.A.. . . . . *83*

CHAPTER 13 **I Am Creative**
By Suniti Saxena, Bed. *88*

CHAPTER 14 **I Am Available**
By Pastor Tim McConnell. *94*

CHAPTER 15 **I Am Able**
By Tyesha K. Love, M.A. *101*

CHAPTER 16 **I Am Unique**
By Marisa Anne Claire *108*

CHAPTER 17 **I Am Balanced**
By Angie Topbas, MBA CHHC *115*

CHAPTER 18 **I Am Light**
By Suzanne M. Gabli *121*

CHAPTER 19 **I Am Positivity**
By Warren Broad, CCHT MFT HAC. *127*

CHAPTER 20 **I Am Loved**
By Evelyn "The Heart Lady" Polk *133*

CHAPTER 21 **I Am Forgiven**
By Tim Eastman *140*

CHAPTER 22 **I Am Me**
By Ashley Love *146*

CHAPTER 23 **I Am Vision**
By Chris Musgrove. *152*

CHAPTER 24 **I Am Recovering**
By Hannah Brennan *158*

CHAPTER 25 **I Am Rare**
By *Amy Noiboonsook* 164

CHAPTER 26 **I Am Understanding**
By *Craig J. Boykin* 168

CHAPTER 27 **I Am Still**
By *Kat Bickert aka Karunaji* 174

CHAPTER 28 **I Am Bridging**
By *Roosevelt "DJ" Standifer, Jr.* 180

Conclusion 184

Foreword

By Robert Ricciardelli

When one has overcome so much in life and then learned how to not only live, but also to grow and thrive, they are now ready to be a special gift to all who they are able to impart to. Nicole Eastman is such a gift, and through her book, *I Am*, she and her collaboration of overcoming voices give the opportunity to encourage and bring practical insights and reflections for transformation to occur to all who read it.

In our busy lives, we often become too busy to reflect and assess what really is going on in the depths of our hearts. What am I really feeling? What do I really believe to be true about myself, and if what I believe becomes my reality, what must I do to create a change in my life?

God has a plan and purpose for your life, and amidst your past or current challenges, the best is yet to come. He has created you for life and for an abundant life of faith, hope, and love for your journey. The first step on the journey of change for yourself is to be aware of where you are, who you are, and to align your thoughts around what God believes for you — and not what you have been conditioned to believe about yourself.

Nicole and her co-authors give you real stories and real examples of transformed hearts and lives. As you read the stories and reflect upon the questions for your own life, you begin to believe the truth about yourself, and you begin to see hope arise once more in your life. Congratulations are in order to all who have chosen to read this book — be ready for an amazing shift in your life to occur.

— *Robert Ricciardelli*

Founder, Converging Zone Network – Principle, Choose Growth.

I AM!

Appreciation and Gratitude

Expressing Thanks

I would like to take a moment to express thankfulness for all who have made this book compilation possible. This has been yet another faith-filled experience, which has proven to show that if you trust and follow where you are being guided, then God will provide and reward you for your faithfulness.

I praise God for guiding me and leading me to all of the beautiful souls who shared their deepest experiences. I have been blessed by each one of them and I trust that You will continue to use each of them and their experiences to bless others.

Also, I am grateful for my husband, Tim Eastman, who has supported me through the time and energy that was necessary for this creation to come to fruition. Thank you for co-authoring your chapter and for allowing yourself the opportunity to step over fear and remain committed to this project and me. I am proud of you for the man that you are growing into and I look forward to seeing how God continues to use your testimony of faith. One day when Jack is older, I know that he will be proud. I love you unconditionally.

Furthermore, thank you to all of the wonderful co-authors of this book. I hope you have some appreciation for the love that I have for each one of you. I do not believe that any of you can fully comprehend just how much you each mean to me. God led us to collaborate together, and I trust that this is just the beginning of our beautiful relationships. My gratitude is overwhelming, as I have been blessed by each of you—your presence in my life, your honesty, your vulnerability, your courage, your wisdom, and your realness. I pray that God continues to bless and reward each of you for being a source of lightness and hope in a world that can be dark and filled with pain; may your days be filled with an abundance of joy and peace in the name of Jesus.

Finally, to all of the sisters that I gained through our time spent together at Hope of Detroit Academy: thank you. You young women allowed me to give, and in return, I received. I learned my heart's capacity to love as you each stole my heart. I love each of you and you will always have a sister in me. I pray that our time together will permanently leave a positive imprint on your lives and that you will always remember just how beautiful you are—God makes no mistakes.

In every thing give thanks: for this is the will of God in Christ Jesus concerning you.

1 Thessalonians 5:18

Introduction

We live in a broken world and people are hurting. Many of these issues of pain stem from our youth and follow us into adulthood. Underneath deceiving appearances and tough outer shells, many, if not most of us, are struggling with feelings of being:

- Abused
- Addicted
- Alone
- Bullied
- Defeated
- Different
- Fake

- Fearful
- Hopeless
- Imperfection
- Isolated
- Negative
- Stifled
- Ugly

- Unable
- Unappreciated
- Uncomfortable
- Unheard
- Unloved
- Unwanted
- Unworthy

Sound familiar? I am sure, because these feelings are common. Even though you may feel like you are the only one who is experiencing the issues that you contend with, you are not. You are NOT alone.

Do you lack confidence and self-worth? It is quite possible that you have never learned to love yourself for who you truly are. Are you held back in life by feelings surrounding body image and what is depicted by society as beautiful?

Maybe you have made choices that leave you feeling remorseful, or maybe you are filled with feelings of regret, guilt, and/or anger. Have you made choices to move forward but are paralyzed with fear? Do you ask yourself, "What if my past were to resurface? What if someone judges me for my imperfections? What if people do not like me for the real me? What if they are mad at me?"

Maybe you have made good choices in life but have suffered at the hands of others. Do you live with a bitter heart filled with hatred? Or do you choose to look past the faults of others and seek forgiveness so you are not held captive by another person's pain?

I AM!

Do you feel lost? Broken? Or maybe you don't see where you "fit in" into this world.

Do you seek forgiveness, understanding, unconditional love, non-judgmental, non-authoritative wisdom, and guidance?

If any of this resonates deep within your soul, then you will love the intimate honesty shared within these pages.

Each co-author has invited you into a place where not many have been. They have opened themselves to you, allowing you into their deepest feelings and experiences. For some, this is the very first time they have allowed themselves vulnerability and healing. Each soul within this book has allowed you to go below the surface; they have shared their experiences, they have provided wisdom gained through hindsight and "learning the hard way," and they have provided practical guidance to help others learn from their mistakes and experienced pain. Hopefully, these honest accounts of real talk will prevent you from experiencing unnecessary pain, and also, allow for the realization that you are not alone.

There IS hope. Recognizing that you are not alone is reassuring. The next step is choosing loving self-talk. There is great power in words and this too provides hope, because you can change your life by learning to speak to yourself positively.

Each chapter title within this compilation is a positive affirmation. Even if you do not feel this way before reading a particular chapter, hopefully you will come to embody each of these affirmations after reading and practicing these words.

May the words that fill this book be a blessing to you and those you love.

Blessings, Love, and Gratitude,

— *Nicole*

Nicole Eastman, D.O.

Dr. Nicole Eastman is a bestselling, internationally published author who turned to therapeutic writing and ministry following a near-fatal car accident in December 2010. Prior to her accident, she earned her bachelor of science in Psychology from Wayne State University and her degree in medicine from Michigan State University College of Osteopathic Medicine. Throughout her undergraduate studies, she worked many jobs, including employment as a NASM and ACE certified personal trainer and AFAA certified group fitness instructor. Currently, Dr. Eastman resides in Grand Cayman with her husband, Tim, and their beautiful son, Jack.

CHAPTER 1

I Am Beautiful

By Nicole Eastman, D.O.

Growing up, I struggled with weight. I remember comments made by family members from as early as elementary school years. Those words left an imprint and hurt worse than those made by classmates. I remember being in Girl Scouts and having to wear a swimsuit around others, and I remember the community shower during sixth grade camp. How uncomfortable I felt in my own skin. I remember hoping for a flat stomach. Beyond the weight, there were the glasses, the crooked teeth, breasts that developed earlier than others, and training bras that brought undesired and embarrassing attention. There were the off-brand clothes and the lack of trendy fashion sense. There was the poodle hairdo (sorry, Mom). Oh, the awkward years. I do not miss them.

I never did feel like I fit in. My emotions were hidden. I was raised to be tough, to suck it up, to fear crying, because "If you cry, then I will give you something to cry for." My relationship with my Dad was strained growing up, as he battled with his own unresolved issues. I always sought his love, his approval, and his time despite our tumultuous relationship. I had always hoped that one day he and I would see eye-to-eye.

My grandma, my mom's mom, was my first mentor. Really, she was my best friend. She was the one who would teach me about what was truly important in life. It wasn't money or materialistic items but rather time and real talk. I treasured those talks around the kitchen table and I told her EVERYTHING. With her, I felt safe. She did not judge me, she listened, and she loved me. Her actions showed me so. When I shared the difficulties experienced at home, she would tell me "You just have to stay strong." When I messed up in life, she would simply share that my choices were disappointing. No beating was necessary, because *ouch!*—those words reached me deeper than any physical punishment could. One day, while sitting and talking at the kitchen table, she gave me a butterfly ring to wear to my high school prom that she'd had from her youth. Two weeks later, she died suddenly and unexpectedly. I learned that butterflies are more than just beautiful creatures; they also symbolize transformation and change.

Following my high school graduation and the loss of my grandma, life took me to college, a gym membership, a love for group fitness classes, certification as a group fitness instructor, certification as a personal trainer, and training for figure competitions, and through all of these experiences—that flat stomach I desired as an overweight child. Through hard work, knowledge, and discipline, my body transformed; and nobody would ever know that I had a daily battle against weight gain.

Once I entered medical school, I had to reprioritize my time. Training for figure competitions and personal training were set aside by my desire to become a doctor. However, my struggles kept me passionate about fitness and helping others, so I developed a program while in medical school to help others with their own weight issues. My passion and motivation grew stronger when my dad's life was taken by a stroke at the age of fifty-three. I was only twenty-six years old at that time, and exercise was my outlet to escape from it all.

Following my dad's death and medical school graduation, I nearly lost my life in a near-fatal accident. Had it not been for my level of fitness at the time of my accident, I was told that I likely would have been much worse off. Other physicians and health professionals attributed my survival to be partially due to my physical fitness. Although I survived, I experienced great loss (physically and psychologically). Hidden disability and pain became part of my daily life. I experienced denial, depression, and anger; but I came to acceptance and healing through faith. God also brought me to mentorship. The time that I spent mentoring the girls at Hope of Detroit Academy is the inspiration behind this entire book.

I AM!

Mentoring allowed me to share wisdom with the young women who became the little sisters that I never had growing up. From day one, we did positive affirmations:

I am beautiful.

My beauty begins in my heart.

My attitude shines through my face with a smile.

I do not need to seek anyone else's approval.

I am confident.

I love myself.

We grew together, gaining the understanding that God created us all—beautiful.

I will praise You, for I am fearfully and wonderfully made;
Marvelous are Your works, And that my soul knows very well.
Psalm 139:14

We talked about body image, models, and magazine covers—the reality of eating disorders, drugs, and Photoshop. Within a forty-five minute mentoring session, the girls went from "feeling ugly" when seeing a magazine cover to realizing their own beauty. All it took was taking photos of the girls and educating them on photo editing; transforming them into an image with flawless porcelain skin. The girls realized that their beauty is real beauty and not the product of art.

During our sisterhood, we also discussed bullying, we experienced the effects of one sister's self-harming cutting behaviors, we meditated, we ate, we laughed, we cried, we loved, we learned, we grew individually and as a whole. Looking back, I see that during those mentoring sessions, I filled the role of my grandma at the kitchen table, and all of my sisters, well they were a younger version of me—insecurities, hopes, dreams, and all.

When God led my husband and me to move out of the country, it was difficult knowing that this mentoring experience (as we knew it) was coming to an end. Although our weekly sessions concluded, our relationships did not. Now, having lived outside the United States, where the perception of physical beauty is seen differently, I have witnessed that "beauty IS in the eye of the beholder." In the United States, people are starving themselves (amongst other behaviors) in attempts to obtain that superficial idea of beauty. In the Caribbean, women are sought out for their curves and a "size two" is questioned for illness. Looking at my own body, pregnancy resulted in me gaining nearly seventy pounds. Thankfully, through knowledge and discipline, I was able to lose that weight; however, my once "perfect" stomach has been left scarred due to an emergency surgery during the delivery of my son. I worked for years to gain that perfect stomach, which I was never fully satisfied with (body dysmorphia); but now, maturity and my experiences gained through my accident leave me with a sense of gratitude. This scarred stomach is a reminder that I was blessed with a healthy and beautiful child—a son who I hope to raise well, who will grow to honor women for their deep God-given beauty.

You ARE beautiful. Do you embrace that?

Our beauty begins in our hearts and shines outwardly. This is a beauty that I could not appreciate during my youth; but rather, this knowledge came with age, wisdom, brokenness, and restoration.

It is my hope for you that you will not experience the pain that I did. I hope that you will learn from my experiences and that you will understand that you were created with a beauty that cannot be duplicated. Do you want to know what truly enhances your beauty?

- Your responses do. When others speak unkind words to you, focus on responding with love. Most often, those unkind words come from a place of hurt from deep down inside of the person who is speaking to you. If someone is hurting you through their words and you respond kindly, then you may be giving them love that they are not receiving elsewhere.

- Your behaviors do. How do you treat yourself? Do you treat your body like a temple? Do you respect your body? Do you insist that others respect your body? There is beauty in self-respect. Proper nutrition, regular exercise, avoidance of drugs and alcohol, and sexual pureness are just a few ways that you can demonstrate self-respect and self-love.

- Your faith does. There is nothing more beautiful than seeing God shine through an individual. You can see it. You can feel it. You can just tell that something is "different" — a good different. I encourage you to grow in your relationship with God. He will never fail you, He will never leave you, and He will always love you.

Now, tell yourself: "I AM BEAUTIFUL." Hear those words leave your mouth, grab onto them tightly, and place them deep within your heart. Repeat these words daily and often until you wholeheartedly embody them. I am beautiful. My beauty begins in my heart. My attitude shines through my face with a smile. I do not need to seek anyone else's approval. I am confident. I love myself.

Anthony J. Soave

Anthony J. Soave has turned a life of diversity into hope and helping others. He has been a truck driver in Michigan and has four children: Noah, Connor, Makayla and Landon. In 2013, Anthony started using his past experiences to help and positively influence others. Through the grace of God, Anthony founded a non-profit organization, Unexpected Blessing, based in the Metro Detroit area, and focuses on feeding and clothing the homeless. This will be Anthony's first book written.

f Anthony J. Soave: http://www.facebook.com/tony.soave.3

f Unexpected Blessings: http://www.facebook.com/pages/
Unexpected -Blessings/1415025342068434

✉ Email: tonysoave07@yahoo.com

CHAPTER 2

I Am Hope

By Anthony J. Soave

The family I was born into, the family I was raised by, is not the family I envisioned I would ever have, let alone turn out to be like. No parent in their right mind ever says to themselves, "I can't wait to have children so that I can raise them in a house filled with yelling, abuse, and alcohol." Unfortunately, that was all I knew. My father was an alcoholic that worked too much. I never knew that this would change my life forever.

Life was not easy for me when I was younger. My mom would make us stay out of the house and go hang with the kids in the neighborhood. I was excited when a teenage kid built me a fort. I thought it was the coolest thing ever. The fort he built was made out of an old refrigerator box, so as an eight-year-old child, it was the biggest fort I had ever seen. The only thing I didn't realize was that my cool fort hideout was about to become my worst nightmare. As we continued playing in the fort, things started getting weird; the teenage boy started touching me. I didn't like it. I didn't like it at all and would ask him, "please stop," but the only response that I would get was "all the kids play like this." I was so excited about the fort I didn't know what to do, what to say, or what to think. This continued on for the entire summer. I was too little, too young, too naïve—whatever you want to call it—to understand what the word *molest* meant. What was happening in the neighborhood was making life uneasy for my family. It wasn't until the kids down the street chased my younger brother with the machete that my parents decided that it was time for us to get out.

After we moved, nothing seemed to change with my father; he just worked harder and drank more. I remember when five o'clock in the evening would come around and my mom would try to prepare my brothers and me for the madness that was about to happen. Growing up in an alcoholic household, you were forced into adapting. Alcohol, abuse, neglect—you learned to adapt or pay the price. My father used to come home in such an angered frenzy, with nowhere to focus his rage on but his own family.

There were days that my dad beat us with a belt from head to toe. Welts covered our body; bright red marks that stung to the touch. Instead of being scared, this was our life as we knew it. There was another time when my dad caught me playing with fire as I started to burn a rag. He got so enraged he held my hand down and burnt my fingers with a lighter, yelling, "How does it feel to be burnt?" The beatings got worse and my father started turning the anger onto my mother. As a kid watching your dad hit your mom, all you want to do is protect her, but you know what he is doing to her, he will do worse to you. My life was complete insanity until mom and dad decided to divorce when I was fifteen.

The things I hid from my family and friends were hurting me, but it was my way of living life. I had to hide things, especially what that boy did to me. I was so afraid to tell my mom or dad. I just knew I would get beaten for it. I became the class clown at school, always getting into trouble. It was my way of dealing with the pain. My life was dark and I trusted no one. I would put on a fake smile and go on with my life, knowing what I felt inside; that all I wanted to do was just disappear from everyone. That was no way for a kid to live, but that was all I knew.

I had so many bad thoughts about myself and my family, but no one ever knew it. I was in and out of trouble in school, but sports actually made me feel like I was a part of something. After a while, I leaned more towards my friends than I did sports. When I was sixteen, my friend and I were having a snowball fight. He ran behind a school bus to give me a white wash and was struck by a car, flew up in the air, and landed a foot from me. He had a closed head injury but survived. Once again, I closed off, held everything in, and didn't talk to anyone about my grief. And once again, it weighed heavily on me. When I was seventeen, I was introduced to drugs and alcohol. I grew up in a house full of addictions but thought I would turn to that. It was fun for a while—partying with friends not having a care in the world, but that all changed the night before my senior prom. My best friend and I were driving like idiots, drag racing down a long country road. In the midst of everything, we saw lights of an oncoming car. He swerved to get out of the lane, lost control, and flipped his car. We all stopped, but when we did, I was roughly fifty yards from the scene. I looked down and saw his shoe. He had flown out of the convertible top of his car and was lying underneath some farm equipment. At this moment, my world was once again completely upside down. When his parents showed up, I remember looking into his father's eyes and not remembering anything he was saying. Knowing the pain we all were feeling, I kept wondering why this happened to such a young promising kid.

At this point, I had nothing left to do but to turn my back on God. God who? He didn't exist. I found a new happiness that would never hurt me, or so I thought—drugs and alcohol. I went down a path for years completely destroying anything or anyone in my path, all because I didn't trust or care for anyone. When I turned twenty-four, while drunk and high on drugs, I was in a fight with another man. He ended up chopping me over the head with a machete and shattering my skull. I was very lucky to be alive. I started to feel that I had a problem and needed help, but I couldn't stop. I started getting in trouble with the law due to being in such rage and taking my anger out on whoever was around me. I was lost.

My whole life until this point was hurt, chaos, and pain. I didn't know what love felt like because growing up, I never felt it. I was always told by my grandma never give up being happy. Never give up hope on what is out there for you. I wanted to just give up, but I always believed some miracle would happen for me. I went to church, I believed in God, but I never understood why He would let this happen to me? Is there a method to this mayhem? Only time will tell, I thought.

A year later, I got on my knees for the first time since I was a kid and prayed. "Please help me Lord," but it wasn't for another full year that I got sober. January, 24, 2003. My birthday. I finally found God, or so

I thought, but once again I was wrong. Being sober saved my life but didn't change my thoughts. Sobriety was amazing for a short period, but after a while, negative things started happening again. I started to question if He was punishing me. I stayed sober, but I was miserable. At the end of 2012, I hit a point where I had a choice: believe or die. God saved my life. I have hurt so many people and myself, countless times, and I had had enough. I started focusing on my faith.

Hope is wishing or thinking something will happen. I always had hope things would get better. Going through all these tough times, I thought I was alone and no one would ever understand me. Never give up on God. He never gives up on us. Things are different now and I realize it is OK to open up and tell what you are thinking. You have to trust in yourself to get your thoughts out and share. Holding things in will only eat you up and hold you back from being the best you that you are capable of. Things that happen to you are not your fault. They don't determine who you are. They help you become who you are supposed to be. Remember, you are young and full of potential. God has a plan.

I AM!

Bernard J. Rabine

Bernie Rabine was born in 1954, and raised in Michigan. At the age of 20, he was diagnosed with Hodgkin's Lymphoma. Bernie has been fighting to live ever since then.

Bernie has been writing since he was in his early teens, writing about courage, going beyond one's limits, and defying convention. His stories are at once, enjoyable, intriguing, and inspiring.

Bernie's premier novel, Barry is a great story about a young man that chooses to face life and death fearlessly.

Bernie and his wife, Colleen live in Midland, Michigan with their three miracle children and a mutt named Scruffy.

✉ **brabine@chartermi.net**

𝗳 **www.facebook.com/brabine**

in **LinkedIn: bernie rabine@linkdin.com**

CHAPTER 3

1 Am Fearless

By Bernard J. Rabine

What is fear? Technically, fear is a series of reactions in the brain triggered by a stressful stimulus and ending with such physical reactions as tense muscles, rapid heartbeat and rushed breathing. Fear stimulus comes in two main ways: A memory of an experience or basic fear; or an imagined fear based on an impression or suggestion. In reality, fear is like an accompanying traveler on your journey. This partner can help you get where you are going, safely or cause you to change directions.

As with many things, you can manage your fears like you would manage someone who is with you on your trip. Sometimes you listen, gratefully to their sounds of warning; sometimes you have to tell them to be quiet and stop distracting you. You are in charge of your journey, you have the right to determine how those people, going with you behave.

Fear does not want to be "managed", it does not want to be silenced, and it does not want to go away. Fear insists that it exists to protect you, and will fight to stay in that capacity. You still have control, though. You still do.

I am fearless because I have spent much time telling my fears to be quiet. Here's an example: When I was in my early teens, our house became infested with bats. We had no idea where they were coming from and we were terrified by them. For many years, we had to deal with the bats. Even after moving away, I was terrified by bats. If I saw a bat flying around in the evening sky, I would run for cover. It wasn't until I decided to study them and then force myself to squelch the feelings of fear when I would see them flying around. I would stand there and watch them, even when they came close, I would tell myself that it was not me they wanted, just some of the bugs flying around. Over time, I have become more comfortable with bats. The fear of them will never go away. I just manage it more readily.

When I realized that I had silenced my fear of bats, it became easier for me to recognize fear as a manageable thing. This realization gave me confidence and power. It can work for you, too.

Being fearless means that you can make decisions that may not be popular to others, but makes sense to you. Being fearless means that you can tell people no, without the sense that they will hate you. Being fearless means that you can pick the people you want in your life, because of what they mean to you, not what you mean to them. Being fearless gives you a raw power that most others do not have. Living a fear-free life doesn't mean you can do anything you want. It means you can make good decisions that will help you achieve your dreams, go where you want to go, see the world for what it is…. opportunity.

As far back as I can remember, I feared not being loved. My father was not a very emotional man, and my mother was a dutiful wife and took care of my three sisters and me in the best way she could. I craved attention and did not receive as much as I felt I needed. That fear drove me to be a busy child, looking for ways to satisfy that thirst for love and attention. In school, I excelled in classes, because good grades pleased my father. But his attention was short lived. I became the "class clown" because of the attention (good and bad) I received from fellow students and teachers. As time flew by, that attention (which I translated to love) became harder and harder to get. It was as if I was hooked on that attention. I felt so alone.

Both my parents did not spend much time helping me succeed. They only became angry when I failed. I came to fear failure, translating failure to not being loved. This tender balance between stepping out to please people and reserving my steps to avoid failing would be the civil war that would rage in me for many years.

Then God showed up.

I AM!

At the tender age of 20, I found out that I had an advanced case of Hodgkin's Lymphoma. The cancer had sneaked its way into my body and began tearing up my digestive tract, groin and underarms. Immediate and radical surgery was necessary to stop the rapid advance. The surgery was a difficult one. Sometime during that procedure, I felt that I was being visited. I felt very warm and incredibly safe. Then a voice said to me, "You are going to be alright." In recovery, I mentioned this to the surgeon. His eyes grew large. Then he told me that I had died during the surgery and the team resuscitated me. I am convinced, at that moment God told me that I was going to live. I didn't think much about it, except that maybe I didn't need to be afraid, anymore, because He had something in mind for me. Because God loved me and would protect me.

After radiation therapy, losing 65 pounds, and much of my hair, I then began to feel that God's words were a heavenly practical joke: yes, I would live, but I would live as a freak. I spun out of control.

Over the next 10 years, I went crazy. I had no morals. The word "no" did not exist in my vocabulary. Girls, drugs, alcohol to the extreme were how I challenged God. Sure, I'm going to be alright. So, I can do anything. I had developed an absence of fear. I didn't manage my fears, I simply lived ignoring them.

Well, God decided He had had enough. So on a sunny, summer Sunday morning after being released from jail for being too drunk to drive. After hitting the bottom, I decided to walk home. The three miles was meant to clear my head and figure out what I would do next. Well, God slid into the fogginess of my thoughts. He told me it was time to start carrying out His plan. Not knowing much more than that, I began putting my life back together. I married a wonderful woman and had three wonderful children. Since that sunny summer morning, I have tried to stay true to His plan. There have been times where I have drifted away from the plan, but He brings me back every time. My faith in Him has allowed me to put away the many fears that have kept me from enjoying the incredible world of marriage, parenthood, and great friends that help me on my journey. Those fears are still there, lurking in the background of my mind and I do my best to manage them. Even though it has been difficult at times, I've never doubted His plan. He knew I needed to hit the bottom, before I could open my mind to Him.

So, what does all this have to do with you? How can any of this have any bearing on what your life is like? It can mean much or little. It is up to you. You have choices. For the rest of your life you will need to make decisions. Big and small. Simple and complicated. Making choices has been a part of your life since you decided to start walking. This will continue until you can no longer understand your options.

Your choices can be based on fear or faith. Basing your decisions on fear will limit what you do in this world. Base them on faith and the world becomes this incredibly beautiful space through which you travel. Your journey is dictated by your choices. All those options include the option of not deciding. This is the most dangerous of options. Your journey is a forward series of steps. Not deciding or not making a choice stops you. You only move forward when you make choices. Some of those choices will be scary. Don't listen to the fear. Tell the fear to go away. Ask God for strength. Then, go with faith.

First steps are always the hardest. They are the most uncomfortable. Each step after is easier. But you must take that first step; otherwise your journey stays in your imagination. Tell the people you want on your journey, where it is you want to go. Those that want to go with you embrace them and move on. Those that do not want to go with you, bless them and move on. They will only hold you back. Then, take that first step and keep stepping, keep going, never look back.

Believe in yourself and the plan God has for you and you too can be Fearless.

I AM!

Vicki Savini

Vicki Savini is a mindful teacher who has been educating, enlightening, and empowering children and adults to be their absolute best for over twenty years. She inspires children to speak their truth and believe in themselves while helping adults to heal the inner child and understand the overall importance of childhood. Vicki is a Science of Mind Practitioner, Reiki energy worker, and talented Intuitive Life Coach. She uses her experiences in psychology, education, and the healing arts to bring out the best in all. Her inspiring book, *Ignite the Light: Empowering Children & Adults to be Their Absolute Best,* will be released May 6, 2014, by Hay House, Inc.

🏠 www.vickisavini.com

f www.facebook.com/TheInfinityFoundation

🐦 www.twitter.com/VickiSavini

✉ vicki@vickisavini.com

CHAPTER 4

I Am Authentic

By Vicki Savini

As I walk down the hall, all I can think about is how light-hearted I feel. I feel so happy and alive. I just left art class and Brett is in that class. It's a win-win for me every day during this period. Art is my home because it's where I feel complete. And Brett, well, he just makes me feel special. For some reason, Brett sees me. He totally gets me and looks at me like I AM SOMEBODY. We laugh together, talk together, and draw together! This is the highlight of my day—each and every day.

My bliss is destroyed as I turn the corner to go to my locker and hear their voices. Suddenly, the pit in my stomach is back. I feel my stride slowing down as I get closer to my locker. I look to see if my cousin is coming down the hall to ease the tension but no such luck. They are there and I have to face their horrible whispers, evil looks, and the dreaded chuckles as either I walk away or they trot away with their ponytails in full bounce! I immediately hear the self-talk.

They are the pretty girls. They live on the hill and have money. They're not like you. They'll have everything and anything they want in this life because Daddy will give it to them. They hate you. All the guys they want like you and they absolutely hate that. They know you're from the other side of the tracks. It drives them insane because you get the attention from the guys without trying. They don't understand it and so they just think you're a slut!

As I make my way down the narrow locker row, I think to myself, "Why does my locker have to be right near their hangout?" The whispers seem to explode in volume like a crescendo as I pass their inhabited space. I try to look straight ahead, but I unfortunately catch a glimpse of their uncomfortable stares. I make a deliberate effort to just do what's necessary and then get the hell out of this hallway, but the laughter begins. My heart is pounding like a jackhammer, my head is spinning, and I feel like I'm going to pass out, but somehow I find strength.

I slam my locker door closed, turn in their direction, and smile. As I walk by, I gaze into their eyes and say, "Hey girls, what's up?" Of course, they snicker and make a rude comment, but I feel empowered because they think I don't care about their opinion of me.

YOU ARE ONE OF A KIND

That was then, and this is now. Back in those days, I was always searching for love and approval from others. I cared what others thought of me because I didn't realize the power that I had within. I allowed myself to be judged easily because I placed my value on the thoughts and opinions of others. I competed in pageants, played several sports, and was involved in just about every club in school—all seeking approval. I wasn't the slut that those girls thought I was. I grew up with all of the jocks, played ball with them in the streets until the street lights came on (unless we kicked them out), and spent time talking with their moms because we were all in the same neighborhood. They were like my brothers. They knew me for who I really was: fun, outgoing, and not afraid to live life. But all those girls could see was that I had the attention they wanted, so they had to make some sense of it by hating me and calling me names due to their own insecurities. Anyone can have an opinion of you. It's truly none of your business. What's most important is that you don't allow their opinion of you to affect who you truly are.

You see, you are one of a kind. You are like a special edition. There is no one in the world quite like you. Sure, you may have some things in common with others, but they broke the mold when you came into this world. Whether you are a twin, a triplet, or just plain ol' you—you are the only version of yourself—so don't try to be anything else. There may be things that you like about yourself and there may be things that you hate about yourself, but my goal is to help you love yourself no matter what you dislike when you look in the mirror. My hope is that when other people say something hurtful to you, that you will filter their words, ask yourself if it's really true, and then make your own choices based upon how you feel about yourself. If you don't like something about yourself then change it. But don't change yourself for anyone else. Only change yourself if you feel a need to be better, stronger, or more inspired.

I believe that deep inside each and every one of us is a light. A bright light that we cannot physically see but instead we can feel. When you are being true to yourself and doing what feels right to you, then your light is shining brightly. When something doesn't feel right inside of you, your light is dim. Our light gets dim when we feel sad, lonely, angry, invisible, and sometimes different. Here's the deal though, different is only what you make of it. Just like there are no two snowflakes alike, there are no two individuals alike either. That's why we are called individuals, so embrace you. Embrace all of the things you like, all of the things you dislike, and all of the things you are unsure of. Learn to love and accept yourself no matter what others may say or do.

LEARNING TO LOVE YOURSELF

I know that it's difficult to ignore the voices that you hear out there in the world, or even in your own head, but it's critical for you to express who you truly are and to ignite the light within. I'd like to give you some tools to help you with this so that you can truly begin to love yourself and be your absolute best. Let's begin...

1. Each and every day, look into the mirror and say, "I love you. I really, truly love you." I know it sounds crazy, but think about how it feels when someone else tells you that they love you. It feels good because it's the approval that you are looking for. Now, instead of seeking this from others, you're going to retrain your brain and find the love you seek deep within. You may giggle a few times and it may feel uncomfortable. Just close the door and look into the mirror. It's just you and the person in the mirror. Don't be afraid to offer that person a few compliments as well (i.e. you're a good person, you're smart, you're kind).

2. When a negative thought comes up, turn it around. (Ex. 1. I'm not good at math—I'm getting better at math every day. 2. No one likes me. I'm a loner—Friends come to me when I am true to myself.) If you allow your negative thoughts to take over, you are simply giving your power away. Thoughts are powerful because they can turn into our reality, so choose your thoughts carefully and only allow the positive thoughts to linger.

3. When you feel that your light is dim (angry, sad, disappointed, etc.), remind yourself that you are loved. Go to a quiet space, put your hands over your heart, close your eyes, and say, "I deeply and completely love and approve of myself." Take deep breaths and repeat this statement until you begin to feel lighter (or brighter).

Always remember that YOU are a one-of-a-kind. You are something special. You were put on this earth to be amazing you, but first you have to realize this to experience your full potential—your authenticity. There's a great picture online that you can find by Googling it to help you remember the power within. Just type in, "kitten looking in mirror sees lion." The caption that is with this picture is, "What Matters Most is How You See Yourself." I encourage you to print it and place it in your locker to remind you to love and accept yourself because you are truly a special edition. You are powerful. You are just beginning your journey of life. The choices you make today will affect the rest of your life, so choose well and choose for you, not others.

For more information and tools to empower yourself, go to www. vickisavini.com or pick up a copy of *Ignite the Light: A Childhood is Too Precious to Ignore*.

I AM!

BrieAnna P. Daugherty,
LLPC NCC MA IMH II

BrieAnna Daugherty is an LLPC, a Nationally Certified Counselor, and an Infant Mental Health Specialist II that practices in the state of Michigan. She works with young people to help them communicate in healthier ways and learn to make safe choices for their lives. BrieAnna studied at the University of Alabama at Birmingham where she earned her master's degree in Counseling and at Western Michigan University where she earned her bachelor of science in Family Studies. Her passion remains in helping young people realize their potential and work to reach their dreams. Today, BrieAnna resides in Michigan with her husband.

🏠 www.YouthCounselingToday.com

✉ brieanna.gesinski@gmail.com

f www.facebook.com/brieanna.daugherty

in www.linkedin.com/pub/brieanna-daugherty/b/a19/a62

🏠 thetruthofmyheartinmyownwords.blogspot.com

📞 (269) 377-3687

CHAPTER 5

I Am Free

By BrieAnna P. Daugherty, LLPC NCC MA IMH II

When I think back to my teenage years, I am transported to a dark, trying, and often painful period of my life. Let's face it, for most young people, middle school in particular is seemingly awful. We are growing physically and emotionally, and yet, many of us feel awkward and don't know what to do with ourselves. We compensate in our own self questioning through seeking material possessions, acceptance from others, and in turn, continue to hide from ourselves. For me in particular, I think back and recognize that I was living my life beneath a strongly constructed mask. I recall moments when I felt so awkward and unpleasant that I would've rather stayed in my bed, under the covers ALL DAY, than at school pretending everything was OK.

On the outside, I think I appeared to be a "normal" (whatever normal is) girl that easily made friends, did well in school, and enjoyed being involved in extracurricular activities. In reality, the only place I felt OK in my own skin was at the dance studio. Ballet allowed me the opportunity to take the emotional turmoil I was struggling with and channel all of the hidden emotions into movement. When I close my eyes, I can still see myself moving, much like a beautiful, flexible willow tree in a rainstorm. Twisting, bending, reaching, and flowing with the environment surrounding me. I can still feel the pounding of my toes in my Pointe shoes on the floor and hear the crackling of the resin on my shoes as I sweep across the wooden dance floor. I can feel the rise and fall of my chest as I breathe in deeply to catch my emotions and channel them into movements. This is the one place that I truly felt like I was honest to myself. I was FREE to be me, emotions and all, when I was dancing. I loved dancing because dancing allowed me to recognize my emotions, validate them, and express them in a healthy way. It was me and nothing about it felt fake, forced, coerced, or uninspired. Ballet, in the end, saved my life.

I doubt my parents had a clue but not because they were uninterested mediocre parents. They were involved, engaged, loving, and all the other wonderful things that good parents are to children. I was pretty adept at wearing my mask, even with my parents. I think back to days I would come home from middle school and my parents were still working. I would slam doors, stomp around, scream, and yell at my younger sister. Hatred spewed out of my mouth at her and then I would just walk away into my room and sob uncontrollably. My body was out of control. My emotions held my body hostage, and I felt like a passenger in a car that was hurtling down the expressway at deadly speeds. I felt countless emotions inside my body but didn't have the tools or knowledge to understand that my feelings were NORMAL. I simply needed guidance in learning how to express emotions in healthy and safe ways. Instead, I kept my feelings bottled up inside, and when they would become all jumbled together and my body had reached "emotional capacity," I would blow like a volcano. Unfortunately, most often, these eruptions were unintentionally directed at my sister. I was emotionally abusive to her because I did not understand what I was feeling and how to express it. I recognized her as someone that loved me unconditionally, and I took advantage of that. This continued for several of my teenage years. Along the way, I now recognize that I had completely lost any sense of self that I had once had. I had become a fragile eggshell that was ready to crack. I continued to stifle my emotions and in turn, accepted mediocrity from myself and others. I lost my voice to stand up for myself and what I believed to be true and morally right in my world. I allowed people in all different types of relationships to take advantage of me and accepted these relationships as face value of what I deserved. I allowed my emotions to continue to build into rage and intermittently explode. Somewhere in the middle of my twenties, I recognized I could not continue along this path. I began to seek help and make amends.

I have since apologized at least three hundred million times over to my beautiful sister for my awful, hurtful, and inexcusable behavior. She,

41

being the person that she has always been, simply stated, "Brie, I knew you were hurting and didn't mean what you were saying. I already forgave you." And so, throughout the years since then, I have spent my time learning to forgive myself, and not only identify, accept, and healthily express my emotions, but also learning to embrace myself whole heartedly with all of my emotions—as part of what God had intended for me. When thinking of this, I am reminded of a quote by St. Theresa of Avila, "Christ has no body now but yours. No hands, no feet on earth, but yours. Yours are the eyes through which Christ looks compassion into the world. Yours are the feet with which Christ walks to do good. Yours are the hands with which Christ blesses the world." Through this journey, I have learned to embrace the divine, which God has placed inside of me. I am learning to love my emotions unconditionally and use them as the gift they were intended to be. This journey has not been any easy one. I have stumbled, fallen, and lain in despair. Through it though, I have learned. I have learned to ask for help. I have sought guidance from loved ones and professionals alike. I have spent countless hours in prayer and endless hours making sense of my world with a counselor. I have learned to no longer fear my emotions. I have learned how to identify my emotions through physical signs my body gives me and through looking more closely at the things going on in my world. I have learned healthy ways to express these emotions and how to use my voice to respectfully express myself to others. Most importantly, I have learned how to be completely free: free from the mask that hid my true feelings for so long. Free to show my feelings openly to others so that they too can learn how important it is to be true to oneself.

For you, in your own personal journey, I offer hope, prayers for guidance, love, support, and freedom of healthy emotional expression. A few helpful tools that might be useful to you are:

- First, know that you and your emotions ARE normal. Remember when you are in a "bad place," it will not last forever. It's a moment on your journey: You are alive, you are feeling, and you are experiencing one more emotion that will shape who you are on your journey in this world.

- Breathe. Breathing slowly and deeply lowers anxiety, heart rates, and helps us to think clearly. I teach clients a "four count breath sequence." Breathe in through your nose slowly while counting to four. Hold the breath for four counts and then slowly exhale through your mouth for four counts. Continue this sequence until you feel a sense of clarity and calm within your body.

- Begin to pay attention to the different clues your body gives you of the feelings you are holding in. Does your heart race and your breathing become heavy when you are angry or anxious? Do you notice that you clench your teeth or scrunch your shoulders up to your ears when upset? Do you sleep way more often when you are sad?

- Listen to your inner voice. Honor your emotions by identifying, accepting, and expressing them in healthy ways. How, you may ask? Identify outlets of expression that help you relax. Do you often turn to music when you feel amped up? If so, try listening to different types of music and spend time exploring how your body and mind feel after you listen to the music. Do you write? Use that as a tool to guide you in expressing your feelings. Maybe you find yourself going outside in times of stress. Go for walks or runs or just BE outside and begin to recognize how your body feels afterwards. Whatever it might be—music, dance, writing, drawing, exercise, spending time in nature, mediation, breathing, etc.—begin to utilize these activities as outlets for your feelings.

- Identify your "safe" people that you can go to in times of need. Go to them when you are scared and confused and ask for help. They love you and want you to find peace and happiness in this journey.

You are beautiful and your emotions are as well. Embrace them and express them along your journey.

Namaste

I AM!

Emily Obukowicz

Emily Obukowicz is an event planner from Seattle, Washington. She enjoys exploring the world, volunteering, telling inspiring stories, and empowering others to live their best life with an open heart. Emily can be reached on Facebook and LinkedIn.

CHAPTER 6

I Am Love

By Emily Obukowicz

Looking in from the outside, people would think that I had it all together, but there was one thing no one knew but me. I didn't know how to unconditionally love myself. The hamster wheel of thoughts that I would think on a daily basis were filled with ideas that I wasn't good enough or even worthy of self-love. This showed up in my life in many ways, as I really didn't have an inner sense of who I was. As a teen, I didn't really know if other people felt the same as I did. I was too afraid to discuss those feelings with other people for fear of not being accepted.

Fast forward two decades later, and I now know that self-love is something that many people struggle with and has nothing to do with age, but awareness of self sometimes comes with experience. I began to ask myself, who am I? I know that I am not my body, I am not my things, I am not my job, I am not my fears, I am not my successes and failures, and most importantly, I am not my thoughts. So take away all these things and what is left? I am a divine infinite soul that was created with Love.

Mahatma Gandhi's quote "Where there is love, there is life" made so much sense to me and really made it so simple. If life equals love, then I Am Love. Being the practical person I am, I wanted to know how I could turn this newfound sense of being to be translated into my life. My lack of self-love showed up in many ways in my life that I knew needed changing: not being assertive, being a people pleaser, not acting upon my heart's desire for fear of failure, self-destructive behavior, lack of self-confidence, and anxiety. If someone hurt my feelings by saying or doing something, I would never speak up and tell that person how it hurt me. I didn't join the drama club in high school for fear of being made fun of, even though it was a calling in my heart. Not having the self-confidence to tell a boy that I liked how I felt about him.

I thought that if I bought the trendy clothes and had the perfect hair, maybe other people would think I was "perfect" and then maybe I would feel better about myself. I gave away my own power by letting other people decide how I should feel about myself. As I entered my twenties, I also let my career and success be the barometer of my self-love. I thought that if I was successful at my career then maybe I would believe that I am worthy of that self-love. The problem with giving away your power to anything outside of you is that it will never be enough. Nothing else can give you that inner self-confidence, self-worth, and self-love. You have to search within to find it within your own heart.

Learning how to love yourself starts with acceptance of who you are in this very moment, even if that person is filled with a lack of self-love. Accepting your lack of self-love, instead of resisting it, actually helps you to move past that emotion rather than resisting what you are feeling. So, something I have learned to do is to recognize the thoughts and emotions that no longer serve my highest self and transform them into an opportunity to love even the darkest parts of me.

I started to say affirmations to myself daily to retrain my brain to accept who I am in this moment. The affirmation I would say to myself daily was, "I love and accept myself for not knowing how to love myself." I would use Louise Hay's method of staring into your eyes in the mirror and saying the affirmation every day. It probably sounds silly, but it's a lot more challenging than you think. The first few times, I would cry and I really didn't believe what I was saying. It felt like I was looking into the eyes of myself when I was a child and how I never felt like I was good enough or worthy. This method really peels back the layers and helps you to get to the core of who you are and accept that piece of you.

As I started to accept myself for what I was, rather than trying to change what I was, I started to feel a sense of relief and that I was loveable for

47

exactly who I was in this moment. I could now look in the mirror and say my affirmation without crying, and I even started to believe that I was loveable just the way I was. The more sense of worth I had, the more I was able to catch those self-loathing thoughts and change them into positive affirmations. As you practice saying these affirmations, you will notice that they begin to be a reflex and you will not feel like a victim to your negative thoughts but empowered by the way you can change them into uplifting thoughts.

Here is an exercise to start to identifying thoughts and emotions that deplete you and how to change those thoughts into empowering statements.

SELF-DEPLETING STATEMENTS	SELF-AFFIRMING STATEMENTS
No one will ever love me because I am not worthy of love	*I am loveable and worthy of all good things in life*
I am so stupid, I don't know how to…	*I am so capable and can do things I choose*
I look so ugly, I wish I was thin	*I am beautiful inside and out and love all of me*
I will never be able to accomplish my goals	*I trust that I am worthy and enough*

Another way that I have been able to connect with my highest self is through meditation. Mediation is a powerful tool that I use to bring me to the peaceful place inside myself where all I feel is love. Using affirmations during meditation is a great way to start your practice. I started for fifteen minutes every morning doing a guided mediation, and I found that it made me feel more calm and that I was able to quiet my thoughts and not identify so much with them. Meditation has also made me feel more in control of myself love and that I can chose to love myself every day and spread that love to everyone I meet. There are many types of meditation and different methods work for different people, but I want to share one way to mediate that has helped me to fully live the love that I am.

I AM LOVE MEDITATION

Sit in a comfortable position where you will have few distractions and slowly begin to breathe deeply. Imagine a column of light that starts from the sun and pours light right into the top of your head. Imagine this white or golden light traveling from your head following through your spine and exiting from your feet into the earth. Imagine the light keeps penetrating through the earth like roots of a tree and finds the center of the earth where the light then bounces back up through your feet and up your spine and rests in your heart. Now as you breath in through your nose, imagine with every inhale that your heart is actually expanding with love and say, "I Am Love." Let your thoughts drift away like clouds in the passing sky. Just repeat the mantra, "I Am Love," as you feel the love in your heart expand.

As you build up your practice, just start with five minutes every morning and then see if you can go to fifteen minutes. The more I meditate and breathe in the divine unconditional love that we were all created with, the more I felt it in my daily life. Learning to love yourself unconditionally is a daily practice. There is no right or wrong way to do it. All you have to do is ask yourself, "What would Love do now?" when you don't know how to heal yourself. The answer will present itself.

I Am Enough

I Have Enough

I Do Enough

I Am Love

I AM!

Judith LeBlanc

Judith LeBlanc raised three children before entering the corporate world where she spent over thirty years working for corporations as an Executive Assistant, then later for several law firms as a Legal Assistant. She also worked for several years as Registrar of a private boarding school for at-risk teens where she was able to mentor young people. Today, she is still in touch with many of the young people she worked with. In 2008, she retired from the working world to design and create jewelry and make homemade scented soaps that are sold online, in boutique shops, and at craft shows. Judith can be reached on Facebook and at judithjewels@gmail.com.

CHAPTER 7

I Am Grateful

By Judith LeBlanc

I know you are going through a difficult time at home and you are feeling that the pain will never end, but it will. I am so glad you decided to talk to me and to trust me with your story.

I understand what you are going through having to deal with one parent with a mental illness and another in denial about the situation. My mother had a mental illness when I was growing up and it only got worse with time. She blamed her unhappiness on everyone around her. No one did anything right, especially me. You are not responsible for your parent's mental illness, or for their unhappiness. You can't make another person happy, no matter what or how much you do for them. Happiness is a decision each person makes for themselves every day.

My father was aware that something was not right with my mother's behavior, but in those days, people didn't discuss mental illnesses. My father's way of dealing with the situation was to become a workaholic and an avid sportsman in order to stay away from home as much as possible. So, I do understand how you feel when your healthier parent refuses to discuss the problem and is absent as much as possible as their way of dealing with the problem they refuse to acknowledge.

The more my father stayed away from home, the more of my mother's wrath was turned toward me, as the oldest child. My mother had no sense of boundaries, so she didn't respect those of anyone else, especially those of her own family members. Your parent with a mental illness doesn't think the way others think. They feel everything is about them or how things affect them.

Your mentally ill parent may make you feel ugly and worthless. That is just their mental illness speaking. I was told that I was ugly and that no one would ever want to marry me or love me. When you are told hurtful things by a parent who is suffering from mental illness, don't listen to their words and believe them. There is no truth in their hurtful words. They are speaking from their mental illness—not from truth.

I felt totally lost in the world of my mother's mental illness, so I understand you feeling lost and helpless. I felt as though my entire life would consist of abuse, and the emotional and physical pain would never end. At school, I was always very quiet, so people thought I was shy. I wasn't shy. I was trying to remain invisible to everyone. I didn't trust myself to get close to anyone at my school. I was afraid if my classmates knew about my situation at home, no one would want anything to do with me. What I didn't consider at that time was that no one had anything to do with me anyway because I was so withdrawn. Because of what you are going though at home, you need friends and mentors more than ever. Your friends will invite you to their homes if you don't feel comfortable inviting them to yours. You need friends to give you a support group. You need a safe place to go to for some peace and a break from what you are dealing with at home. And you need God to get you through the bad times, keep you strong, and give you hope.

Right now, you probably feel there is no hope. There is always hope. You have to believe that whatever you are going through, you can trust God to carry you through it until you are old enough to change your life and your situation. Then you can use your experience to help others. There will come a time in your life when you will feel grateful for all your experiences, even the bad ones you are going through right now, because they will help shape you into the strong, faith-filled, compassionate person you will become.

I am thankful that these days any type of mental illness can be comfortably addressed and not swept under the rug and hidden from the light of day. You can never heal what is hidden. If I'd had one person, one adult who I could have discussed my home life with at that time, it could have helped me more than anyone could imagine. Allow yourself a support group of close friends and adult mentors—people who know how special you are, and who not only believe in you, but help you to believe in yourself.

I'm not certain what your relationship with God is, or if you even have one right now. At the time I was growing up, I formed my concept of God by my parent's treatment of me. I thought of God as a vindictive bully who made rules no one could possibly follow all the time and who just waited for you to break one of His rules. Then He was going to enjoy punishing you.

I was so wrong in my concept of God. When I was a little older and more mature, I discovered that God is a loving, nurturing father who wants only good things for us in life. A father who is forgiving and merciful. Who wants us to be successful, happy, healthy, and filled with joy. A lot of the unhappiness we experience in life comes from not trusting Him or understanding His great love and mercy. We bring a lot of it on ourselves by the choices we make. Even when we make bad choices, if we turn our situation over to Him and ask for His help, He can turn things around and make something good out of the mess we made for ourselves.

If you have ever considering or ever do consider ending your life as a way to end your pain, please understand this, ending your life does not end the pain. It just stops you from living a life that can be filled with joy. You could be on the brink of something wonderful and joyful happening tomorrow. But if you are not here tomorrow, you will never know what that is. You would be missing God's plan for your life.

You will get to a point where you are able to forgive your parents. My father passed away a few years ago. I blamed him for not protecting me against my mother's abuse and for being sometimes physically abusive himself. I thought he should have controlled her. Now I realize he was as much a victim as the rest of us. He couldn't control her any more than I could.

My mother and I were estranged for many years until she was elderly and in a nursing home. When I learned she was in a nursing home, I decided I needed to forgive her and establish contact with her again. I wanted to give her the opportunity to leave this world in peace, knowing she was forgiven and had nothing left to be settled where I was concerned. I was surprised to discover that forgiving her set me free. It was as if any ghost of the control she ever had over me vaporized the moment I forgave her.

We still had things we could never talk about due to her total inability or unwillingness to deal with her own mental illness. Our conversations were very superficial. She was never willing to allow herself to be happy in life, and eventually, reached the point where being unhappy was her comfort zone. She still blamed everyone else for her unhappiness. But her children finally realized that they were not responsible for her happiness or her unhappiness. Her problems didn't have to become our problems. We didn't have to fix anything that was never ours to fix. She did reach the point where, even though she couldn't face facts about her own mental illness, she was able to tell us that she loved us very much. In her own way, I'm sure that was true. And for the first time, I believed her.

I understand that right now you feel completely lost and hopeless, but you won't feel that way forever. Realize that you are not responsible for another person's happiness. You can only be responsible for your own life, your own happiness, and your own actions. Believe that your life will get better once you are out of your current situation, and in time, you will be out of it. It won't last forever.

It is important that you are the one who can break the cycle when you are ready to start your own home and your own family, so the cycle of dysfunction and abuse can never affect your own marriage and children in a negative way. You can take your power back and use it in very positive ways. You can build a wonderful life for yourself and your family.

Have courage, have faith, and trust that God can and will turn your circumstances around. Wake up each morning with an attitude of gratitude. God has a plan for each of His children, and it's a wonderful plan filled with life and joy. Hang in there long enough to discover what His plan is for you and your life. Then live it, and enjoy every minute of it.

I AM!

Kimle Nailer, BA

Ms. Kimle Nailer, founder of Positive S.I.S.T.E.R.S., is committed to teaching women the importance of experiencing their inner essence as the expression of their beauty. Her passion for supporting women evolved as a result of her experiences from childhood, into her mid-thirties, of living with low self-esteem, before discovering the power of transformation that came from her reconnecting to her inner essence. Today, she is a successful heart-centered Entrepreneur, Dynamic Speaker, Best-Selling Author, and Spiritual Intuitive Life Coach, and uses her own life story of overcoming low self-esteem to mentor youth and inspire women to live from their heart. She has become known as the "Alchemist for Soul Awakening" due to her work of helping others find their soul's purpose, from their painful memories of the past and early childhood programming, so they can successfully transform their lives into confident visionaries, capable of building their lives, businesses, and their communities. Ms. Nailer speaks regularly at women's retreats, conferences, schools, corporations, and various organizations.

You can connect with me at:

I AM!

🏠 www.positivesisters.com

ⓕ www.facebook.com/mypositivesisters

🐦 www.twitter.com/positivesisters

CHAPTER 8

I Am Present

By Kimle Nailer, BA

You may or may not be familiar with author Eckhart Tolle's book, *The Power of Now*, and the truth he shares about being present, and the power of living in this present moment, right now.

Right now, as you are reading this book, how present are you?

Being present is a sacred gift because it allows you to be in tune to your feelings and to know yourself. It is your gateway to feel love. Unless you are present in your heart and mind, you lose the ability to intuitively guide your life to its highest potential. Access to this powerful "knowing" allows you to know your heart's desires, know your purpose, and know love for yourself and others.

There are many distractions that keep us from being present. However, the main reason most of us are not present in our hearts is because we have detached due to painful experiences. In this chapter, I would like to welcome you home to reconnect with your heart, past the pain and into being present.

As a young child, I detached early from being present in my life due to the pain of being a little black girl born in 1963. The climate of America didn't foster many opportunities if you were black, and even inside the Black Race, there were "light-skinned" privileges not afforded to those of us with darker skin. Unfortunately, I was black before black was beautiful, so as a young girl, I never received the compliments like I heard given to my sisters who had fairer skin. I was often teased and called names like "ugly black monkey," "black tar baby," and words I can't include, destroying every ounce of self-worth I had as a child. Can you imagine the pain I felt as a little girl, never being called pretty or cute?

During school, I only had one friend from kindergarten to fifth grade. I was content with my only friend, because I was teased regularly for being dark-skinned. At age eleven, I went to a small Christian school in Ohio, secluded in Amish country in an all-white community, until I graduated high school. During that time, I lived in total seclusion from the world, without television or radio, clueless about how the world operated. Now, not only did I have dark skin, but my family were the only blacks in the entire school. That created another level of isolation, because although we were Christians, I was never invited by my classmates for sleepovers, or asked to sit with them during church. I would hear about the weekend activities the following Monday. At one point, I did ask them to include me, but that lasted only a short period. Here I was again with no friends, always trying to fit inside a world that had no place for me.

While my siblings played outside, I spent my time reading, the place where I found solace and comfort from the world I didn't fit inside. I explored distant places and lands, learned about people in other places, and interacted with the characters in the stories as if they were real. Sometimes I didn't know if I had experienced it, or simply read about it. When I read, I felt I had complete control because there was no one to judge me, so the world I lived in felt less painful. I had concluded my place in the world was limited and a lonely journey, so I had few expectations for myself. I simply floated along in life, wishing I had lighter skin. Being from a large family of ten, and the eighth child, made it easy to get lost in the shuffle, without any personal identity. My life was lonely, and the only joy I experienced was from my reading or going to church.

Fortunately, at eight years old, I had an experience with God's love that began my Christian faith. As a Christian, it was easy to follow the rules of my faith. After all, there wasn't much I could do, having dark skin. My mom was a devout Christian and minister and prayed for us during the night, many times in the wee hours of the morning. I would often cry as she moved on to one of my sisters to pray for them, because I knew if I could pray like that, I could keep this presence.

It wasn't until I was much older that I realized how detached I was from my heart. Desperate for love and validation made me willing for any relationship that promised love, even if it was not fulfilling to my soul. I decided to date a man that I really didn't feel a connection with, but I was mesmerized by how he felt about me. I relocated to Chicago, IL, and become engaged, only to have that relationship deteriorate. Three years later, I returned to Detroit, MI, after ending the relationship in depression, over twenty-five thousand dollars in debt, and broken in my faith. After months of therapy, medication, and counseling, I learned that my desire for love and validation prevented me from the ability to have healthy boundaries in a healthy relationship. I went along with whatever he said to feel his love.

This experience transformed my life and opened a whole new world to me. As I began to reconnect to who I was, I learned that my value of myself determined how present I was. I learned that self-esteem is critical for every young girl, teen-ager, and woman because it determines how she sees her worth and becomes the basis from which she will interface with the world. It determines what she believes about herself and impacts how she relates to peers, chooses careers, selects partners, builds relationships and friendships, cares for her body, cares for her health, and most importantly, how present she is in her own being.

I'd like you to think of self-esteem as a cup or container. The larger the size, the more present you are of your being. And the more present you are, the clearer you will be of your life's purpose. Sometimes you have to grow you, the container, to become more present with yourself—as I did. The greatest example of growing myself was when I decided to go to college at thirty-two years of age, embarking on a new journey. It was this experience that built my confidence, made me know I could have dreams, and opened my life to my worth and value. I found untapped passion and experienced the power of loving yourself enough to dream.

I want you to know that you can rebuild your self-confidence and value without external validation. I accepted myself for who I was and allowed my inner essence to define me. I now share who I am with the world, versus being controlled by the opinions of others. Before

61

becoming this new woman, I aimed to please everyone for validation. Now I love myself, and I choose to be me, including my dark skin, and so can you. I now live from my heart, my desires, and my passions because I'm present with my inner essence. Now I love the woman I have become, and I pray you will embrace who you are, also.

I know now that painful experiences don't have to define you, or cause you to detach from being aware of your being. Over time, you may have lost aspects of yourselves from painful experiences. But I welcome you home to be present again. So how do you find that reconnection?

My detachment from myself happened over time, with each rejection and teasing. The pain caused me to slowly lose connection to my heart, thinking I was not good enough. The lost hope, love, and faith slowly erodes a part of our beings away, leaving us to believe we can't have the life we want. You don't have to relinquish yourself to the power of the painful situation anymore. But have faith in God, and reclaim yourself to pursue your dreams or aspirations of your heart.

If there is no one home to dream for us, how can you live a life of purpose? Who can feel your presence? God wants to give us the desires of our hearts, and He will heal your heart to receive those blessings. Allow Him to enrich your heart with new desires or passion, so you can you live a life of purpose.

Maybe your struggle was not your skin color but some other aspect of your body, or from another painful experience that made you believe you were less than loveable. There are three things I want you to know: 1) You must love yourself; 2) You don't need others to validate your greatness; and 3) Know your worth because of what God said about you.

To support your reconnection with your soul's essence and become present in your heart, download my free copy of "9 Keys to Unleash Your Soul's Essence" at www.unleashyoursoulsessence.com/offer.

We can live by God's promise, which says, "In my presence is fullness of joy"—unspeakable joy!!

Welcome Home to Your Heart

Para-Chaplain Michelle Smith

I began reaching out to incarcerated youth in 2004 with a Christian non-profit organization called Pacific Youth Correctional Ministries, based in Orange County, California. I graduated from California State University of Long Beach with a teaching degree and went on The World Race: an eleven-month overseas backpacking mission trip! After returning from that faith-building journey, I became a Para-Chaplain with PYCM. I've dedicated my life to helping rescue teens caught up in the gang lifestyle, running the streets, and those behind the walls of juvenile hall facilities. Setting captives free in Jesus's name!

f www.facebook.com/michelle.smith.169067

⌂ www.pycm.org

CHAPTER 9

I Am Valuable

By Para-Chaplain Michelle Smith

At thirteen, I committed to wait for marriage. I knew I didn't want to give myself to just anyone. I wanted to honor God, my future husband, and myself. I had no idea how difficult a fight it would be. I can do all things through Christ who strengthens me! Nothing's impossible with God. Today, I'm still a virgin, twenty years later. Waiting has taught me to value myself. Sadly, the world unashamedly tramples over purity. Our bodies and hearts are the greatest treasure: we need to protect them!

You're more precious than silver and gold. There's just one of you, which makes you extraordinary and special! No one walking this earth has your unique fingerprints. You're the only person who can live out the destiny God has designed for you. His thoughts of you outnumber the grains of sand.

Realizing your value is a process. We believe it when we start to grasp the depth of God's love for us. If you don't understand that you're made by God for God, then life will never make sense. My thoughts about myself, God, and others shape my life, in a positive or negative way. Seasons in my life simulated roller coasters, steered by emotions and feelings of fear and disappointment. It would've been a more peaceful journey if I was grounded in God's truth. Lessons in life taught me that my value comes from Him; not from my looks, possessions, the amount of money I make (or don't make), or what other people think.

Looking in the mirror, I wasn't always happy with what I saw. I didn't feel comfortable in my own skin. Insecurity was my middle name. In my late teens and early twenties, I believed that if I starved myself, I'd be more beautiful and accepted. It was Satan's nasty lie. That belief became a stronghold in my life, and I hid this secret from everyone. My distorted view of my body and beauty resulted in destructive choices as I battled anorexia on and off for a few years. I grew tired of the effects of mistreating my body. I knew I had to stop, or else it would cost me my health and life. God reminded me that I was perfect how I was, no plastic surgery needed. I didn't have to be stick thin, or a certain size or shape, to be attractive. Charm is deceitful and beauty fades, but a woman who fears the Lord shall be praised! Inner beauty's more valuable than outer beauty. I began eating healthy, working out regularly, and accepting myself. We can be our worst critic. Do you see yourself through God's eyes? Ephesians 2:10 says, "For we are God's masterpiece. He has created us anew in Christ Jesus, so we can do the good things he planned for us long ago." Daily, I need to remind myself, "I am valuable. I'm God's flawless masterpiece!" Think it, say it, and believe it!

I'd like to say that after conquering anorexia, I never questioned my value. But that's not the case. Stubborn me went through another rough lesson: My heart was shattered, crying in the dark parking lot. I trembled in fear, anger, humiliation, and hurt. His footsteps grew distant as he fled the scene, leaving me stranded. I stared at my phone and knew what I had to do…

Yet, I couldn't bring myself to press those three numbers: 9-1-1.

Thankfully a friend called the police for me and let me stay overnight to recover. The police arrived, questioning me. Tears ran down my face and I thought, "I feel worthless, I am nothing." Depressed, I hit a low point. It was the last time I'd allow my fiancé to assault me. Yes, my fiancé, the man whom I met in church and thought I was in love with. He would tell me, "I love you," and then push me to the ground in a fit of rage.

I told myself, "This is the final time he's going to hit me, threaten me, and talk down to me! This isn't love!" Hurt people hurt people. He claimed he'd change, but his actions didn't match his words. He put on a charming face for everyone, but behind doors he took his anger out on me. Ten years later, I've never received an apology for the damage he caused. The blame always shifted on me. Even though I was faithful, I felt like nothing I did was "good enough." I still have scars from that experience. God gave me strength to forgive my abuser and I filed a restraining order for my protection. Forgiving someone doesn't mean you're excusing their behavior or remaining in a harmful situation. Forgiveness frees you from bitterness. The quicker we forgive, the sooner we're healed. I stayed in that relationship for a year because I didn't realize: I am valuable!

In Matthew 22:37-39, Jesus replies, "You must love the Lord your God with all of your heart, all your soul, and all your mind. This is the first and greatest commandment. A second is equally important: Love your neighbor as yourself." He's jealous of our hearts and wants all of us, not divided leftovers. He values His marriage with us! He's our Groom. The desire for affection, security, attention, and companionship lead me to "worship" men as my idol in my twenties. I'd be focused on serving God, working, and college…and then a handsome guy would show interest in me. I'd convert to "distracted, party of one!" I've lost count how many times this disturbance derailed me. Thankfully, He allows us to approach His throne of grace and get back on track. The safest, most secure place to be is in His strong arms. He's our protector, provider, and Lover of our soul.

For two years, I worked at group homes for abused and neglected teenagers, and my Lord broke my heart for the fatherless troubled teen population, opening my eyes to those desperately crying for help. I grew up with loving parents, so witnessing victims of neglect ruined me for life. I was determined to stand up for injustice and be a voice to the voiceless. I grew up in Orange County, California, but I was sheltered from the thousands of gang members and incarcerated youth. They were out of sight and out of mind. I never dreamed one day that I'd be excited to hang out with gang members in dangerous alleys and teens in juvenile halls! Now they're my favorite crowd to spend time with. I fell passionately in love with the outcasts of society, like Jesus did. I saw my Lord's grace for me through them. We've learned inspiring lessons from each other. They've taught me just as much as I've taught them. I've never felt so close to Jesus as when I'm feeding a homeless person or visiting an inmate. Society labels groups and tries to dictate who's "acceptable and worthy" and who's excluded. God sees every life as valuable. I never "did time" behind bars, but I was imprisoned by my own destructive thoughts, emotions, and rebellious behaviors. Jesus set me free from those chains, and now I've devoted my life to help set others free.

I started volunteering with a Christian non-profit organization called Pacific Youth Correctional Ministries in 2004. After seven years of faithfully teaching bible studies in the units, I joined the Chaplain team. This meant living off 100 percent donations and serving the youth-in-crisis fulltime! I've discovered my calling and want to spend the rest of my life reaching out to gang members and prisoners. I want to be the person who reminds them they're valuable, speaks life into them, calls out greatness in them, and proclaims His Gospel. I want to point them to the Healer and raise awareness, letting the world know "these youth are valuable!"

Olivia is one of the precious teen girls whom I've had the honor of mentoring the last few years inside juvenile hall facilities. She wants to share her words with you: "This is my eighth time being locked up. I didn't believe in God. I've struggled with drugs and finding my value. I'm a kind person who's been taken advantage of a lot, used by "friends," and thrown away. I was introduced to the Lord and Michelle when I got incarcerated. I started going to church, praying, and reading the Bible for the first time. I promise you that when you're at your lowest, you can sit and pray with all of your heart and the Lord will be with you. He loves you with all of His heart. He'll never leave. You should never feel alone. God saw me in my cell and knew I was feeling sad, so He brought Michelle to share His Word, laugh with me, talk, listen to me, and lift my spirits. I'm learning my life has value because of Him."

Never forget that YOU are valuable!

I AM!

Samantha Smith,
MSc Psych., BSc Psych., IANLP, MBPsS

Samantha Smith is the founder and senior counselor and psychotherapist at Therapy Matters Counselling and Psychotherapy practice, Manchester, UK. With over a decade's experience working within healthcare, she has developed a deep interest and understanding in human behavior and adaption. Samantha is a master of psychology, an NLP practitioner, and psychotherapist. As a member of the IANLP and BPS, she works ethically and passionately. In her personal time, Samantha enjoys being a mummy to her two young children and runs a group for parents/caretakers of special needs children to support, share, and socialize together.

🏠 www.therapymattersmanchester.co.uk

✉ contact@therapymattersmanchester.co.uk

f www.facebook.com/therapymattersmanchester

🐦 www.twitter.com/TherapyMattersManc

📞 07583 449 162

CHAPTER 10

I Am Worthy

By Samantha Smith

Wouldn't it be wonderful to fall in love with ourselves as we do others, to feel a love and respect so strong that we'd do almost anything to make ourselves happy?

Growing up in a home with both my parents still happily married, after meeting and falling in love at age fifteen, I felt proud. I saw how hard they worked at their marriage, and I never once doubted that I would have that same experience with my first love. Looking back, I guess this was quite naïve, seeing as the majority of my friends' parents were separated. But for me, well…Love is supposed to be forever, right?

What I never thought about was how I defined love. Is it that gut-wrenching, knotted stomach? Having your every thought consumed by that one person? Trying so hard to be the person they want you to be? Or is it that invisible connection with someone who understands and loves even those parts of you which aren't so desirable? Someone who makes you laugh until your belly aches?

What I did know is that the former never made me feel too good, feeding anxiety and stress, whilst the latter made me happy and content. I wish I had stepped back from the hormones and whirling emotions and asked myself which of these was good enough for me. Now I know.

I fell in love with a friend. He was older than me, not particularly handsome, but rebellious and complicated. He spoiled me rotten. He thought my friends were childish but said I was different, older than my years. I felt the need to prove I was grown up enough for him. He made me feel good about myself. Before I knew it, I had grown away from school friends. They made plans without me. When I questioned them, they said they thought I was spending all of my time with him instead. They said he made them feel uncomfortable…awkward even. He insisted they were jealous of us, and over time, friendships grew distant, and we both became a little bit more dependent upon what we had.

A year passed, and he grew paranoid, made comments about the things I wore, told me my knees were knobby, and I shouldn't wear skirts. I was impressionable and horrified at my knobby knees. I swapped my school skirt for pants or thick black tights. I would wear two pairs of jeans to hide my shape. I became self-conscious. I wore makeup to make myself look nice for him, but the harder I tried, the less he seemed to care. "Get that sh*t off your face," he'd scold me. Then I realized he must care, because he insisted on meeting me every lunch break. He came out of his way to walk me home from school. Even became angry when a boy from my class spoke to me. Is this caring? I sometimes felt stifled and alone. Other times, I felt special that he cared enough to want to be with me all the time. He was scared to lose me, so much that when I tried to spend some time with my friends, he said he'd make sure we died together rather than me leaving him. I felt threatened. Then he bought me gifts and I decided I was being silly.

Over time, he gave me very good reason to feel scared. At this point, I was so isolated. Yes, I had my family, but I felt they wouldn't understand; they struck lucky first love. I felt like I'd failed. I wasn't enough for him. I didn't reassure him enough. I angered him. I broke his rules by accident. I simply didn't satisfy him.

I had put so much energy fighting against my parents, trying to prove our love was real, telling them that this older boy was a good guy and treated me right. How could I possibly tell them they were right? It felt too hard to admit. It hurt.

Meanwhile, he flitted between bombarding me with endless love letters and gifts, to threatening and following me. My friends, who he had made feel uncomfortable, were now spending more time with him than I. He was older, cooler, he bought them alcohol and cigarettes.

71

I AM!

It would have been easier to stay with him, but I realized my worth. My dreams. My sadness. I wanted more.

I trusted a family member and they helped me stay strong. I soon realized that this was not love but infatuation and control. It was time to make a choice: Did I want to feel this way, or did I want a chance at true happiness? I knew at this point I wanted to give myself the chance I deserved. The chance we all deserve. I wanted to feel loved, pure love which helps us thrive, encourages, and supports us without ultimatums, and with plenty of mutual love and respect.

This was the first positive step I took in a series of events which had led me to suffer a serious, life-changing attack and settle for a number of unhealthy relationships. Although I broke free and took the steps in the right direction, and for this I am very proud, I did not at this point realize my worth, acknowledge healthy boundaries with others, or have the confidence to seek the support I needed.

So, I wonder what I would say to my younger self. Firstly, I would congratulate her on her endurance, her courage, her realization, and newfound self-respect. I would wish for her that she had found it sooner and had set down healthy boundaries within both relationships and friendships. Strong, firm boundaries. I would tell her how she is worthy of a love which makes her feel proud and confident and that if she feels the need to be someone else to keep another person happy, then she is spending time with the wrong person. She is a gift and she must recognize this.

I would ask her to fall in love with herself so much that she would only pursue the best for herself and those around her. To accept herself and others for what they are whilst knowing the difference between forgiving peoples' wrongdoings and allowing them to be done to her.

I would ask her why she treated herself more harshly than she did others. Why she didn't realize that she is equally precious, equally beautiful, and equally worthwhile.

I would ask her to repeat the following facts on a daily basis and to hear the truth in every word.

I am worthy.

This is who I am.

I have the courage to fight for my happiness.

I allow myself to feel love of a true kind. My own love. I will love myself truly, and I will share my love with those who respect my differences and embrace our lives together as a team.

I AM!

Shannon Monticciolo-Davis

Shannon Monticciolo-Davis was raised in a close-knit community called St. Clair Shores, Michigan. Though she loved her small community, she had visions of a bigger community she acted upon. After graduating from Michigan State University and marrying her husband Joe, she moved to Prosper, Texas. Using her small town personality and her gift to gab, she spent ten years consulting companies and showing them how to grow their businesses. Through hard work, Shannon was able to become a director of business development at a world-renowned ballet school. Though Shannon misses her small town back home, she has established her own community through others that have been adopted.

🏠 www.iamwanted.org

🏠 www.facebook.com/wantedbyadoption

CHAPTER 11

I Am Wanted

By Shannon Monticciolo-Davis

There were three days that changed the path of my existence. The day I was born, the day I learned the details of my adoption, and the day I married.

On Christmas day, when I was eight years old, I was told I was adopted. At such a young age, I never really thought much of it and led a very normal life.

Fast forward to the age of fifteen:

It was a beautiful summer day in Michigan and a friend of mine came to my front porch, where us girls always hung out, and said: "You know you are adopted right?" I said, "Yes, so what of it?" She started explaining that her mother told her I have a family member who is actually my real mother, I was born addicted to drugs, and I was never supposed to be born. There goes a bombshell!

Imagine the shock and anger I felt hearing details from a friend and not my own family? Fifteen years old and the sunny warm world I knew became instantly gray. I knew I had to talk to my parents. Once I did, the gray became black. I felt completely and utterly alone.

During that traumatizing conversation with my parents, I was told a past that was kept hidden from me for fifteen years. My existence consisted of an abortion that went wrong, hospitals, drug addiction, the possibility of having AIDS, the physical fights, the courts, kidnapping, to family stress and depression. Above hearing all of that, these were the words that were said to me that I will never, ever forget. "You see, nobody wanted you. They wanted your brother but not you. What could we do? We couldn't just leave you naked on the street. Nobody wanted you, and we really didn't have a choice." Bombshell number two. Nobody wanted me? I have a brother? After the conversation went on for about three hours, the words that came after were very blurry. No matter how much explanation was given, I could not get those lines out of my head.

I felt I was taken in as a favor, in pity. Why was I still alive? Why did my biological parents not want me? Did my adoptive parents truly want me? Where was my brother? Did he know about me? Was he having a good life? How could they leave a baby on the streets? Why did they choose my brother over me? What could a helpless baby do wrong to anyone? What did I do wrong? Why was I so bad?

At fifteen, you are just starting to learn about yourself. Before I knew of this history, I always felt alone as it was. My family loved me dearly and the best way they knew how, but I always felt somehow or someway I was there in pity. I always felt extra eyes looking at me, as if there were people always talking about me. At least I can say I now know why — people were. Everybody knew of my story except for me.

Hearing this news of not being wanted absolutely sent my emotions into a spiral — something I never fully recovered from until I started a family of my own.

I never had the right type of support to help me through my emotions. My parents had to deal with this ordeal for five years, hide it from me for the next ten, and somehow heal from their experiences. They had enough of their own emotions to work through before trying to talk about it to me.

Growing up, we kids were raised in the strict traditional Italian household. Where the motto is, "Look right, act right, speak when you are spoken to…" and never talk about your emotions. Every day, I was hurting, and every day, my parents were hurting, but we never talked about it. Actually, they never talked about it. It is not until today, as a grown woman married and with child, that my parents and I have a conversation about it.

I AM!

If only I could go back in time and talk to myself. What could I say to myself to get me out of my dark hole? What could make me happy again?

If I could go back, I would say: YOU ARE WANTED. You have always been wanted. God has always wanted you.

People, especially when emotions are high, have a terrible way of expressing themselves. Your parents and family have always wanted you, even if they just didn't know it at that moment. God had a bigger plan for them and for you.

There are many different ways to view the world: through the eyes of the suffering, the hurting, and the negative or the fighting, the recovering, and the hopeful.

Here is a fact: This world has sunny days, and there are days when it is cloudy. Though it may seem as though the world is always dark and dingy, the light always shines through. It was God's promise to us.

Many paths I could have taken when I got that news. In fact, there were times where I would try to purposefully sabotage my life. I would spend countless days feeding into the negativity that surrounded me. At the age of nineteen, I knew I needed to make a choice: be the person everyone expected me to be, or be the person that I wanted to be...to be the fighter I knew I had in me.

I could have been swept away by the nothingness I felt towards the world. I could have been consumed by the stories of abandonment and betrayal. But at the end of the day, I made the decision that they needed to become just that: stories. With all stories, you can always change your ending.

To be adopted means that God had a wonderful plan for you to be raised by people he handpicked for you. Being adopted is something to be proud of. Being adopted automatically makes you strong. You will have challenges with finding yourself, but it is OK. Everybody has the challenge of finding themselves. It is OK to feel alone but know that you surely are not. It is OK to forgive those who hurt you. They are hurting themselves. You did nothing wrong to deserve what life threw at you. There is evil out there in this world that will try to make you doubt yourself and what it feels like to be loved. There are hard days ahead that you will endure without the help of friends and family, but you are never alone. God has always wanted you. The pain and suffering can end if you change your path.

Do not let the past cloud your future. Always look for the light through the clouds. Above all, do not let others cloud your judgment, as they have not seen the light through their own cloudy day. Communicate your feelings to a friend, a family member, a counsellor, or somebody you trust. There are great people out there, but you have to find them. Change your path and know your stories can be rewritten into something beautiful.

My story of adoption rewritten:

I was adopted. God chose a wonderful family who provided and protected me from harm when I needed it the most. God chose a family who loves me for who I am (regardless of my blood type) and who I became to be. God knew that the family he chose for me was the best fit for my future and me. God had a plan for me from the beginning. He used another vessel in order to ensure his vision was proclaimed for me, and as a result, my happiness. Since I knew I had him on my side, I knew he could take my uncertain beginnings and turn it into a life of love and hope. By being adopted, I was able to learn about me. I learned I am able to see love without heritage, without color, and without restrictions. Through adoption, I am able to not know but trust I am in good hands.

My biological parents had their own path to follow. My adopted parents had their own path laid in front of them that they followed. Now I must set my path and follow it. I must follow this path because I am wanted by God.

I AM!

Sheilah M. Wilson, MA

Sheilah M. Wilson, MA, is an extraordinary Transformational Life Coach, entrepreneur, teacher, author, and facilitator of mindfulness exercises, guided imagery, and energy psychology techniques. She is a Licensed Professional Counselor, Licensed Independent Substance Counselor, Certified Master Addiction Counselor, and Board Certified Coach. Sheilah has accumulated more than thirteen thousand hours coaching clients to achieve transformational results. She is brilliantly insightful and intuitive, respectful and compassionate. Sheilah has a diverse background of experience and expertise that grounds her in the unique position of being able to awaken, catalyze, inspire, and champion a diverse population who come to her with a variety of issues, blocks, needs, desires, concerns, and goals. Sheilah works hard to be as healthy as she can be mentally, emotionally, physically, and spiritually; this heart-centered commitment allows her to be the best possible coach and mentor for her clients.

⌂ www.sheilahmwilson.com

✉ info@sheilahmwilson.com

I AM!

www.facebook.com/SheilahMWilson

www.twitter.com/SheilahWilson

www.linkedin.com/in/sheilahmwilson

Instagram: shemoth888

CHAPTER 12

I Am Heard

By Sheilah M. Wilson, M.A.

Growing up in a dysfunctional family is not very rare these days. Unfortunately. But as a teenager, I did not really know how disturbed and unhealthy my upbringing was—or maybe I DID know and could not face the truth. After all, what could I do about it? Fire my parents? Disown them? Run away? Kill myself? These were certainly all options I considered at one point or another. And maybe more than once.

My father was physically abusive only toward my sister. Watching her being beaten at the dinner table for being a picky eater took its toll on me deeply; I was traumatized observing her trauma. I became the "good girl" who always finished eating everything on my plate, even when I was not hungry, or already satisfied and full. As a result, I lost touch with my true appetite and became an overeater. Food became my best friend and allowed me to stuff down all the fear and angry feelings I was not permitted to express. Sadly, at the time, I did not know or understand this was happening.

My mother was chronically depressed and yelled at us daily. She was mean, cruel, unkind, and uncaring. She had grown up in an abusive family herself and thought she had "cured" her dysfunction by going to therapy for several years. I never saw any improvement in the way she treated me, however. She remained emotionally unavailable; my emotional and spiritual needs were never met. I felt invisible, not seen or recognized for the unique being that I am, and certainly never heard. I stopped trying for fear of being hit for allegedly being "disrespectful" for speaking up, and I sank deeper into my unhealthy relationship with food. When we are young and do not understand these things, we can

83

only make sense of it by deciding, "There must be something wrong with me. I am broken, I am flawed, and I am ashamed of who I am, or I would not be treated this way." It was painful growing up in the chaos and terrorizing moments, not knowing if my mother would hug or hit me each time she approached. I walked on eggshells. And many years later, when I asked my mother why my younger sister got everything she asked for, she replied, "You never asked." How convenient! Scare me to death, shut me down from asking for my needs to be met, and then accuse me of not getting what I needed as if it were my fault. That's crazy-making stuff! When I asked for her help or support, she would say OK or make promises and then deny she ever agreed to be there for me. Now that's really crazy-making stuff! I grew up second guessing myself, wondering if I had imagined the promise, buying into and believing other people's reality of what I was feeling or needing, and staying confused and uncertain most of my life.

There are worse stories out there, extremely dysfunctional families, and greater tragedies than my story. But that is not the point. We are each individuals with varying levels of sensitivities and needs that parents are supposed to recognize and respond to. It is of no value to try to compare ourselves to others. What is important is that we each begin to unravel the lies and self-deception and take back our power to get our own needs met, somehow, some way, hopefully functional and healthy.

So I began to write, draw, dance, sing, run, and play to escape the torture of my teens. At night, lying in bed, listening for footsteps to our bedroom, my sister and I would wonder if mom was coming in to yell or beat us. I was scared all the time on the inside but appeared calm and capable on the outside. I became a great actress. The only recognition I received was at school, and even then, that was challenging to maintain with any consistency. My sister got the straight A report cards; I did not. I became more social, always looking for acceptance and approval. Everyone needs to belong, feel heard, and be recognized.

So I prayed. I was raised in a Jewish home without formal religious training. But by the grace of God, I somehow knew there was something greater out there—and inside me—that would listen…and care. After all, I thought I was a good person—kind, gentle, sensitive, talented, cooperative, caring. That had to count for something. Someone had to care. But why were these things happening to me?

I believe that the greater the soul, the more challenging the life here. Whether you agree with that statement or not, it is important to practice trying to separate YOU the person from what is happening in your life—those are definitely two different things. And to conclude that "bad things are happening to me because there is something wrong with me" is totally inaccurate. Poop happens—it is how we learn to deal with it that defines our character and determines our mood, thoughts, and behaviors. Please remember you always have a choice in the moment of how you want to show up in the world. I am not suggesting you pretend you are fine all the time; it is good to feel ALL your feelings as they arise and acknowledge how you feel: "I am angry." "I am so disappointed." "I feel lost and confused." What is so interesting about allowing all the yucky feelings to be accepted is that when we are present with these feelings, rather than ignore or push them away, they seem to go away on their own. Like you, all your feelings just want to be heard. Listen and let them go, or watch them go away as you observe the difference between you, the amazing person that you are, and the feelings. These emotions are simply "e-motions" or energy in motion. Practice letting the energy move through you as you notice how you are feeling. This is a core practice of mindfulness—being present and aware, in the moment, without judgment. We learn compassion this way, for ourselves and others. What could be greater?

Being in my body did not feel safe as a teen and young adult. Now I can feel when I am hungry and when I am satisfied. I am present and I listen to ME! It is MY voice that I can now hear, respect, and from where I take all heart-centered action. It took a long while to get here, but I chose to practice and develop the skills necessary to learn to listen and be heard by the one person who I could rely on, who really cared—myself.

But what about God and my prayers? I know today without a doubt that there is a loving God who deeply cares about each one of us. That does not necessarily mean our prayers are always answered (in the way we want them to be answered). There is a larger plan at play here, and I have learned to trust the timing and unfolding of the grace that comes into my life. The point is that it will and does come! The timing and how it looks is not up to us. Every challenge, tragedy, and disappointment I have lived through has brought me great gifts I could not have imagined (or even prayed for).

If you do not yet believe God is there for you, listening to you, that is OK, too. That will come in time as it did for me. The power of the spoken word cannot be denied. You know how it hurts when cruel and unkind words are directed your way; similarly, when you speak loving, thoughtful, gentle words to yourself and others, it has the opposite result—goodness, well-being, peace, and acceptance. Those are the feelings we usually seek when distressed, angry, and upset for any reason. Affirmations are a fabulous way to begin this journey of learning to listen to yourself, start to feel better, and own the truth of who you really are! Here are just a few suggestions to start:

God doesn't make junk. (Just look around at nature, newborn babies, the sky...)

I am a divine spark of creation here to express my individuality and the unique gifts I have been blessed with.

There is only one me.

I am on the wrong planet—this planet is not fair, but that doesn't mean there is something wrong with me.

I honor the power I have been given to choose to be happy right now, even though _____ (fill in the blank with whatever is going on, such as "this person said or did this," "I screwed up," "I am angry," etc.)

I love you even though we have never met, because I see the goodness and preciousness of all creation in you. It is so, and you are heard! Blessings for your courage to stand up for yourself, even silently, as you grow in confidence that all is in Divine Order.

Suniti Saxena, Bed

Suniti Saxena is currently working as an Art Teacher at Christ the Teacher School, Fort Lee, NJ, and is a US Citizen. She holds a degree in Arts and a degree in Education. Recently, she has started Creative Wonders, weekly arts and crafts classes for kids to help kids develop their uniqueness and original ideas. The purpose of her life is to work for children, especially girls. She has a variety of artistic interests. Her innovative mind is full of ideas. She looks forward to contributing her modernized designs of kitchens, dishwashers, furniture and cars.

✉ sunitiuniq@yahoo.com

📞 2015771020

✉ ssaxena@christtheteacherschool.org

✉ suniticreativeworks@gmail.com

f www.facebook.com/sunitiscreativeworld

CHAPTER 13

I Am Creative

By Suniti Saxena, Bed

I am creative to love and protect the creation of only one creator, God, who creates love and life and their food to live. He gave me brain, wisdom, and intellect to understand my right to love myself and understand the duty to protect and improve the quality of life of His innocent creation — CHILDREN — who are dependent on the adult world.

Through my art and creativity, I am on my way to show:

ART RELAXES RESTLESS MINDS, ENABLES US TO EXPRESS IN DIFFERENT WAYS. OUR OWN CREATION GIVES US THE FEELING OF SATISFACTION AND CONFIDENCE THAT CLEANS AND ENHANCES OUR INNERMOST SELVES

And I teach:

ART IS A COLORFUL EXPRESSION OF THOUGHTS AND EMOTIONS

BELIEVE IN YOURSELF AND IN YOUR OWN ART

ART IS A FRIEND WHO IS ALWAYS AVAILABLE, WHEN THERE IS NO ONE TO LISTEN OR UNDERSTAND

YOU ARE THE INTERIOR DECORATOR OF YOUR OWN HOME

When you rearrange or decorate your room, you exercise your mind, along with rest of your body. You set your room according to you — and your room, your home, becomes your heaven.

Feel the beauty of art, and while creating, feel God's gift of ability in us. And while constructing, you will feel the presence of God, the giver. Art and construction comes from peaceful mind. To achieve peace in mind is not that easy. We need the support of our family, teachers, school, and friends. Destruction comes from the devil that is in the mind too, but not so easy if good morals are being built from the beginning through art.

I experienced that when we use our brains in constructing something original, not copied, it opens our brains and we feel like we are exploring. It makes us happy and we develop positive confidence. After constructing, the next part is decorating to make our piece beautiful. And while decorating, we think about colors, looks, appearance, balance, and harmony, and negative thoughts start disappearing.

Who am I? I came to know when I passed my childhood, teens, and early youth—the three precious stages in the whole life span.

Why didn't I believe people who showed me appreciation and praise in their eyes? Going back to my teen years, during my summer holidays, I wanted to wear new fancy and stylish outfits while going out with my girlfriends every evening. Once, I sewed a purple dress with a flare made from my mom's silk sari (Indian traditional outfit), falling on my thighs and over my knees. I went out like I was going to a fashion show. One lady in our neighborhood commented, "Nice pattern." Another day, soon after waking up, I started collecting rags and pieces of satin bedcovers that we stopped using because we preferred cotton. Combining those rags, I ended up turning it into a fancy top before that evening to go out and show. I should not have been friends with those girls who commented sarcastically, "Suniti wants to wear everyday a new outfit, no matter if she completes it or not. She doesn't care even if one sleeve is yet to be sewed." "Ha, ha!" they laughed at me. And I believed them, not the lady who praised me about the nice pattern. I believed something was missing in my childhood. Was it confidence and self-esteem? I knew my talent but also knew that I could not pursue it. Modeling was not accepted in the family I was born. Fashion designing was not affordable. Though my father was working as a civil engineer, he was the only bread earner with a family of three children, and he was suffering with acute asthma, and my mother had high blood pressure.

Also, I knew that any one career in art could never satisfy me. I was allowed to decorate my shared room with my sister, only after asking my mom. She never liked whenever I tried to decorate our living room. But I was stubborn in this matter. I kept making artistic pieces to put on our living room's shelf, because that was the only way to show the guests or visitors.

I still remember my sculptures that I sculpted from mud I used to dig out from the playground and that sculpture of a man, proudly decorated on that shelf. When my mother saw, asked me, "Is that a sculpture of your husband? Why do you waste time on these things? Study, take a job, and go to your home. Decorate your own home, not this one." In India, daughters are considered to be guests in the home where they are born. They don't inherit their father's property. Many families have changed and follow the law to give them equal part in their will. But the mentality is same. Sons are pampered, daughters are not. Very few daughters are lucky to be loved by their parents, but still, sons are the head of the family after their father's death. This behavior makes the boy child possessive from the beginning. In our family, that was extreme. My sister accepted this, but I never did. I always argued. I developed a soft corner for my younger sister because she never argued, so she never got she wanted.

I recollect another incidence of a sixteen year old me with a restless mind and many boundaries for girls. I started enjoying writing as self-fulfillment and to express myself—pretending and acting in the privacy of my room—creating my own pretend world. I started writing during the nights.

When my mom saw this, she snatched my novel—80 percent complete. I wanted to disclose only after completing it. No doubt, God gave parents their rights to their children, but that was not a decent way, staying up to see if a teenage girl's eyes were open or closed. I pretended to sleep, tightly and forcefully closing my eyes. How could I sleep with so many thoughts in my mind? How could someone lock my eyes for the night? I felt ashamed, as if I wrote something wrong. Negative thoughts started coming in my mind, and I was not able to sleep. I had lost my confidence in almost every sphere of my life. One morning, after struggling to sleep, I got up from the bed and burnt my pages and decided never to write again. I was forced to take sleeping pills to be able to sleep properly and on time. I was not able to concentrate on anything. Those pills were giving me false sleep. I was sleeping every night, but in the morning, I felt more tired than fresh. Why didn't my parents understand that, while we are able to do many things on time, sleep is a natural process? Sometimes, creative artistic minds full of ideas can't rest or sleep until expressing them. If we keep lying in the bed without sleeping, it makes our body more tired, and our whole body aches. Sometimes, three or four hours of natural sleep is better than eight hours in bed without sleep. I was not confident enough to go anywhere by myself. I was not feeling better, even after taking medicine. I never agreed with medicine to lead my life. Believe it or not, I gave up all my medicines without telling anyone. Arts and crafts became a magical meditation and worship to me that brought me closer to God.

Later in my life, some peaceful people hugged me, encouraged me when I was feeling low, and were like God's messengers in human bodies.

In accordance with my father's wishes, I became a qualified teacher. I was determined to find my true self, so I continued concentrating on my interests while creating, exploring and writing short poems. I made white fabric doves to cover shoes when they were not being worn, to remind me to go always towards peace and to burn the gold in me to shine, to find the diamond in me. I was mature enough to wait for a husband who could understand my art. And a man came like morning after a long dark night. I painted morning. We married. I am in the US because of him. He believed in me and in my art and bought me canvases. He bought me clay. He let me do everything I wanted to do in the area of art.

Now I have to perform as a mom to my daughter and provide her everything that a mother can, so that she has no regrets, no repenting in the future when she is on her own—A GROWN UP!

While concluding, I have to say that I know you believe in God. So trust him. Everything happens for a cause and God created us, no matter what country is a part of His only one world, so you should have the confidence and guts to say that you don't follow any culture, any tradition, any belief that your heart and mind don't allow you and that delays your progress. God wants you to live in His world without fear, keep creating for advancement, without harming others or yourself, approaching towards Him with love.

Pastor Tim McConnell

Tim is an Ordained Bishop with the Church of God.

He has served in ministry for over twenty years, as associate pastor, evangelist, and teacher, as well as serving as chaplain for a local chapter of the Royal Rangers boys club.

His compassion is mentoring and seeing other young men and women achieve great success in life, believing every individual deserves greatness in life.

Above all, Tim is a husband, father of three daughters, and grandfather of six grandchildren, and believes that his love for his family must be priority.

✉ **www.mcconnellt@hotmail.com**

f **www.facebook/Tim McConnell**

📞 **(864) 423.3239**

CHAPTER 14

I Am Available

By Pastor Tim McConnell

I saw it in her eyes, weariness of being a young single mom with two young sons, working overtime to make ends meet, and the frustration of not being able to help her oldest son, now twelve, was bringing her to her breaking point. She reached for my hand as she and her boys were leaving church service that morning and timidly asked if I had time to talk with her son, Teddy. I knew it was urgent. I could feel her small hand tremble as she held my hand. I agreed to meet with Teddy that Sunday afternoon before the evening service. She quickly responded with a thank you. As they left the parking lot that morning, I whispered a prayer for them and began to pray for wisdom when we met later that day.

The Wade family had been attending our church for a little over two years. Barbara had been left widowed after the tragic death of her husband. She was now left to raise two young boys, full of life — Teddy had just turned twelve and was in middle school; his brother Tommy, two years younger.

These boys were country boys, for sure. They loved playing in the woods, wading in creeks, and discovering new things about nature every day. It was common place to see them find two limbs that had fallen from nearby trees and watch them pretend to sword fight.

Teddy was small for his age, but I was sure he would one day have a growth spurt, but for now, his brother Tommy and most of the other boys his age were much larger. Teddy was a cute little boy, finding out that being small was tough, especially in school. He wasn't afraid to use his mouth to defend himself, which often landed him in more trouble than he bargained for in the end.

As I arrived early for my counseling session, I opted for the use of our church youth room rather than the pastor's office. I felt it would be much more personal and maybe ease his anxiety. As Barbara and her sons arrived, I greeted them at the door and asked them all to come into our counseling session for a few moments. I explained to Teddy that his mom and brother would be across the hall in the sanctuary if we needed them. Security means very much to young people in counseling.

"So how has your day been, Teddy?" With his head down, he replied "OK, I guess." "How's your fort coming along, Teddy?" As his head quickly snapped back, he replied excitedly, "It looks great, Pastor Tim. If I could find some more building material, I should be finished soon." "What does it look like? Tell me about it!" Teddy sat straight up in his chair and began using his hands and arms to describe the unique design of his fort.

After letting him tell me all about his adventures for a good bit, I asked him, "Teddy, aren't you afraid of bears out there in the woods?" And he replied, "No sir, I ain't afraid of no bear or snakes, but there is just one thing that I'm afraid of." "Really, and what is that one thing?" I asked. Teddy, with eyes wide open and hands in the air replied, "Spiders, I hate them; they are creepy!" I smiled and said, "Teddy, I hate those little creatures, too!" He asked surprisingly, "You do?" "I sure do. You see, Teddy, sometimes even little things in life scare us adults, too!"

As Teddy became more comfortable with our conversation, I began to ask him about his incident at school and found out that bullying by other kids was a major problem.

Let me offer some suggestions to young boys without a dad that they can talk to in this situation:

1. Don't be afraid to talk to your mom, but also, talk to your Youth Pastor or adult male leader in your church.

2. Don't feel like you are a loser or less important because you have been bullied.

3. Never allow your anger to cause you to hurt others because you have been hurt.

4. Realize you will grow up and find a male mentor that you want to be like and ask them if they will be your big brother.

Having to live a man's life with sometimes adult responsibilities in a little boy's body isn't fair. Little boys and young men should get to enjoy their youth.

Find a church that offers programs that will allow you to interact with qualified adult males in programs, such as "The Royal Rangers," or other male mentoring ministries.

There are many men that are willing to love and support you as a young man and see that you learn new skills and grow spiritually, mentally, and physically by providing activities that you will enjoy. You will enjoy camping, fishing, hiking, and other skills that you will retain for a lifetime. Friends will be made and teamwork will be a necessity as you grow up, and your leaders will model this consistently before you.

Having goals in life will become important for you, and being awarded for your achievements will give you great confidence throughout your life.

Trusting an adult mentor/leader is difficult when you have never had an adult male involved in your life, but you must begin with a limited trust, and as your relationship grows, so will your trust. Never feel like there is no one that you can trust or confide in. It is a lonely world when you feel that you can only trust yourself.

Don't be afraid to ask your mentor questions, even if they seem simple. Good mentors love questions and will do their best to provide you with the correct answers.

Always be honest—usually that's all most great mentors require. For a mentor to help you, you must trust him and he must trust you. Even if it hurts to tell the truth, the consequences of telling the truth far outweigh the guilt and consequences that follow a lie. Honesty is a must!

Realize within the heart of your mentor, no matter how old, is the heart of a young lad. No young man ever learned skills in life without it being modeled or taught and passed down by a mentor. Ask them to teach you and help you do things that you like to do. Most grown men enjoy acting like little boys again.

I believe the most important relationship that you can have in life is with Jesus Christ. Realize that all people are not perfect, and though we try, we often fail and hurt each other, but Jesus Christ will never fail you or disappoint you or leave you. He is always available for you—anytime, anywhere. Don't feel alone another day; receive him as your Savior today. It is as simple as this prayer:

Dear Jesus, I am a sinner in need of a Savior. I was born a sinner and need salvation. I receive you today in my heart, believing that through the redemptive power of your blood you shed on Calvary, it cleanses me from my sins and the power of your resurrection grants me eternal life. I receive by faith my salvation in the name of Jesus Christ, my Lord. Amen.

Returning to my story in the beginning, I guess you probably wonder how Teddy is. It's been two years now, and Teddy has grown, not so much physically, but a whole lot spiritually and emotionally. His mom, Barbara, is now married to a wonderful Christian man that has stepped up to the plate to become Teddy and Tommy's dad. Teddy is so happy now. I was honored to perform a portion of their wedding ceremony and those boys couldn't stop smiling. Their stepdad spends time with them, as well as two of his own. They recently came by our home, and to see the joy in Teddy's life, and the change it is making, is unbelievable.

It's sad that not all stories end like this, but if you are a young man searching for a mentor, there is a Christian man praying somewhere that God will use him to impact a young man's life. As he prays God hears his voice as he says, "I'm available."

Don't give up on your search, but beware, you will not find God's finest man in sinful places doing sinful deeds. Ask God to lead you to a mentor, and God will cause your paths to meet. Just remember, when you are older and successful in life, return the favor, pay it forward, and invest in a young man's life. There will be one searching for you.

Will you be available?

I AM!

Tyesha K. Love, M.A.

Through Tyesha's personal experiences with adversity and triumph, she has dedicated herself to encouraging people to walk in the truth of their struggle. Her accomplishments were made through faith, persistence, optimism, humility, and self-belief.

Tyesha Love's professional background in business management and supervision, coupled with her educational acumen in Organizational Leadership, developed her skill set to assist in strengthening individuals, teams, and organizations within various controlled settings. Her mission is to lead, develop, and motivate people while passionately promoting awareness and empowerment; engendering inspiration and motivation; and nurturing personal and professional development, amid inspiring vision and direction.

Tyesha K. Love
200 W. Butler Ave
P.O. Box 872
Ambler, PA 19002-0872

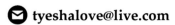 tyeshalove@live.com

I AM!

🏠 www.tyeshalove.com

🐦 www.twitter.com/lovetk78

in www.linkedin.com/pub/tyesha-k-love/21/72b/a94

CHAPTER 15

I Am Able

By Tyesha K. Love, M.A.

Despite the challenges I have faced, and will face in life, I have realized, I Am Able.

All my life, I felt I was targeted by God, the "enemy," people, and situations. I grew up feeling like the black sheep of my family. I seemed to constantly be faced with challenges. And I also struggled with a lack of self-esteem and self-confidence. I looked for acceptance from—and aimed to please—others to feel loved. Looking back, I realized that in those low and tough times, life was shaping me into the woman I am and continue to grow to be.

Some of the challenges I faced were from decisions I made without the thought of consequences. Included in those choices were getting pregnant while in high school and running away from home. Other challenges were simply life's happenings. In either instance, how I respond to those situations means a significant difference between succumbing to the struggle and triumphing over them.

As a teen parent of two children—my first child at the age of seventeen—all around me were doubters. I knew I had made my life challenging by having children at a young age. Raising them was not done with ease. Conversely, in May of 1997, I graduated from Germantown high school with my children, Taylor and Joseph, looking on as I accepted my diploma.

Raising children as a single parent and making a life for us came with great hardship and much hard work. There was also reward. However, I used both the negative and positive as motivators. Those that doubted me — "friends" and family members, seeing peers get pregnant, drop out of school, and become comfortable waiting on a check from the government motivated me to do what I needed to provide for my children and myself. Although I temporarily needed financial assistance, I strived toward no longer depending on the system to provide for my family. I refused to listen to those that believed I would become "just another statistic." Fast forward eighteen years, I look back at my accomplishments. I went back to school and furthered my education earning a master's in Organizational Leadership. (I am proud to say that my children were there for that graduation, also). I have been employed and caring for my children since 1999. I purchased a home in the suburbs where my children could attend one of Pennsylvania's top ten school districts. I purchased the car I always dreamed of having and, in a few months, I will witness my children graduate from high school. I am able to beat the statistics and reach the goals I set for myself.

In the matters of relationships, I had a pattern of having always sought love in all the wrong places. Perhaps it was to fill voids, the fear of being alone, or simply failing to acknowledge that I was dating down because I did not want to feel lonely. I realized I entertained unhealthy relationships. I realized that I engaged in relationships that had no real foundation. I wasted time in relationships where there clearly was no future.

I also came to realize that I needed to learn to be comfortable being alone with me. In that alone time, I grew mentally, emotionally, and spiritually. I grew in self-love. I would enjoy my hobbies, have "pamper myself" Fridays, and, occasionally, take myself to dinner and a movie. It is in those times my spirit is most calm and mentally rested. It is in those times I feel at peace and am able to clear my mind and feel closest with God.

I learned how to love me first. In growing in this self-love, I learned my worth, re-evaluated my values and standards, and identified what I really wanted out of a relationship and friendships. I can now love and be loved fully. I am able to recognize the patterns, re-evaluate matters of the heart, and in my life, address issues regarding self-esteem and confidence, and learn to love me first.

When I was diagnosed with breast cancer at the age of twenty-nine, I thought that was the universe's ultimate kick in my behind. I dealt with fear and surrendered to the disease. I had complications that put me in the hospital for days at a time. Actually, my thirtieth birthday was spent being admitted into the hospital for a weeklong stay because of lethargy and an infection at the reconstruction sites.

Being twenty-nine and told 1) you have breast cancer, 2) you need a bilateral mastectomy with the option for reconstruction, and 3) I have a genetic mutation, BRCA1—which puts me at a high risk for developing certain cancers or high risk for a recurrence—is a big pill to swallow. I was inundated with emotions of denial, acceptance, anger, optimism, grief, doubt, fear, and feeling alone in the world of cancer. I was discouraged by setbacks. Yet, I was uplifted by faith, hope, family, and friends.

As I find writing therapeutic, I wrote journal entries about various experiences throughout my season with cancer—treatment, surgery, healing, and the plethora of emotions. I vented about how cancer strained relationships and caused emotional, financial, and relational distress. I exposed the unspoken words that follow a cancer diagnosis.

My memoir, *I Am Not My Hair, A Young Woman's Journey and Triumph Over Breast Cancer*, is a raw and authentic telling of my season with cancer. I chose to take the negatives that came with my cancer diagnosis and make it a positive to inspire and educate others. I share my personal testimony to engender awareness and to give others hope. I am able to survive. I am able to encourage young adults to educate themselves on proactive and preventative measures and encourage them to learn their family's medical history and to be advocates for their health.

For those things over which I had control, do I wish I had made wiser decisions or thought things through more thoroughly before acting? Of course I do. Do I have any regrets? I have none that I can think of. I have learned the importance and impact of forgiving myself when I make a mistake or fail. I allow myself to feel the emotion in that moment and move on. I also pride myself on learning from experiences and mistakes and not repeating them.

I AM!

Even up to this day, I refuse to listen to anyone that may doubt my abilities, especially when I put my mind to something and set a goal, and if it is something for which I have passion. I surround myself with positive people who uplift my spirits. I make sure that when I set a goal, it is not to prove something to someone, but that all my goals are mine and not for the approval or acceptance of others.

What makes me able to rise above personal and professional challenges and overcome disheartening obstacles? Since as far back as I remember, I was always one to ponder how I could make the best of a situation — what could I learn from it; build from it; improve the outcome of? After some self-discovery, I came up with a personal mission statement. A personal mission statement provides a sense of purpose. It helps define who you are and how you will live. I sought out mentors and accountability partners — people that would speak only the truth and offer constructive criticism. These are people with whom I have a foundation of trust and respect. I built relationships with like-minded people and people who inspire and make me want to continue to grow professionally and personally.

I am able because I believe in myself and the vision for my future. I unwaveringly hold onto my values. I am able because I dream big and without ceasing. I am able because I work hard, because nothing good comes easy. I am able because I take risks. I am able because I am dedicated to my goals and strive with perseverance. I am able because I live for that in which I have a passion. I am able because I am humbled by each challenge, period of growth, and each accomplishment. I am able because I plan and visualize, evaluate and adjust as necessary.

I am able because of the support from loved ones — my children being my biggest motivators. I am able because I share of my gifts and blessings. I am able because of my faith in God, for using the tools which He has provided me, and because I follow the direction in which He sends me. I am a model for overcoming adversities.

"Every problem brings you a gift." Author unknown

Embrace adversity. Focus your energy not on the problem, but on finding the gift within.

For more inspiration, or to connect with Tyesha, visit http://www. tyeshalove.com or pick up a copy of Tyesha's memoir, *I Am Not My Hair, A Young Woman's Journey and Triumph Over Breast Cancer.*

I AM!

Marisa Anne Claire

Marisa Claire graduated from M.U.D. MakeUp Designory, Burbank, California, in 2003 as a certified Mastery Makeup Artist. Although makeup is a passion, she returned to her previous banking career for several years, completing a decade of total service until 2010, when she was laid-off. Her son, who was born in 2008, whom she has raised on her own, was almost two years old at the time. Losing her job was not only unexpected but also life-changing. Realizing the economy had drastically impacted the work environment, Marisa decided to go back to school to pursue another passion—ASL. American Sign Language had been Marisa's language in high school, and she used baby sign language with her son before he could even speak, so that he could communicate his needs and minimize frustration. She graduated in 2013 with her associate's degree and continues to pursue her bachelor's degree toward licensure as an ASL Interpreter.

CHAPTER 16

I Am Unique

By Marisa Anne Claire

It's so easy to compare ourselves to others—her hair is perfect, he is great at sports, why can't I be like them? It's been pounded into our heads that everyone is different, and that's a good thing, yet we are surrounded by standards and ideals. Look at the people on the covers of magazines—aren't we being sent a message that this is the image we should strive for? What a confusing world we live in! The goal is to not let all the idealism around us become our own personal standards. Your standards need to be what's right for you, the uniquely perfect individual that you are.

My struggle was to find a balance of acceptance (the things I cannot change) and still achieve MY perfect (change the things I can). My perfect is different than your perfect or anyone else's perfect. "Perfect" is what is appropriate for you. I'm 5'7". I think it would be much cuter to be 5'4", but I can't change that—being shorter is not my perfect. However, I have brown hair, and I'd rather it be blonde—that I can change. It's like one of my favorite sayings: "pick your battles." Don't set yourself up for failure and choose ideals that are unattainable. YOUR perfect must be realistic. Please never compare yourself to others—it is only fair to compare yourself to God, because that is where true perfection is found. There is no picture of God to compare our physical appearances to. God's perfect is about values and morals— what's on the inside, heart and soul. Sometimes the best things you can change about yourself in order to achieve "your perfect" are internal, not external. Another favorite saying I have is that everything happens for a reason and there are no mistakes. That's because God is perfect.

Trust that what you see in the mirror (your external) is not a mistake. We are all beautiful in our uniqueness.

Just because we are all different does not mean that we are disconnected. You are part of an eclectic species that shares common experiences, thoughts, and feelings. Just because you don't look like the person sitting next to you doesn't mean that they don't have the same interests or haven't gone through similar struggles. Being a unique individual does not mean that you are alone in your individuality. Trust me when I say that there is definitely at least one person out there who gets you. I understand that sometimes finding that person can be a challenge. Be patient and trust—easier said than done, I know. You will find a kindred spirit one day, if you haven't yet. Cultivate a relationship with yourself, your Higher Power, God first, and then the rest will fall into place. When you love yourself, others can't help but love you too.

Maybe now, you're wondering, "How do I cultivate a relationship with myself, God, my Higher Power? How do I find MY spirituality?" Whether raised religious or not, you must find a spiritual path that rings true for you. Try the following and see where it leads you:

1) Learn the art of meditation. My belief about meditation is not to strive to do it perfectly, but just to do it at all. Sit (or lie down) as still as possible. Begin to notice your body—feel your back against the chair or bed, your toes touching the ground or sheets, whatever sensations you recognize, just be aware.

Next, I like to ground myself and connect to Mother Earth. Imagine a cord of light from your feet reaching way down into the center of the earth. Now, just ask for guidance and clarity. Feel free to ask a question. The tricky part is not being attached to a particular answer or outcome. Just quietly breathe and wait to see what images, thoughts, or feelings come to you. This is your Higher Power communicating with you. You've begun to cultivate your relationship with God, the Universe.

2) Start a journal. Journaling was (and still is) a huge outlet for me. Writing down your thoughts and feelings allows you to begin to see on paper who you are, what makes you tick. When you go back and read journal entries, you get insight and inspiration. You might just be surprised how much you can learn from yourself by writing.

3) Love yourself! Look in the mirror and think in your head "I look good today!" I used to spend hours in the bathroom. Laughably, my father thought I was doing drugs, but in actuality, I was playing around with makeup and hairstyles. I was getting to know the physical me. That was just as important as getting to know the emotional me. Yes, we've all heard that true beauty comes from the inside, but self-esteem comes from accepting what you see in your reflection. You don't have to look like a model to feel good about yourself. All you have to do is wear your favorite shirt or style your hair in that way you think is so cute, and BAM you feel good, right? Find your favorite physical attributes and focus on them. Stop the negative self-talk about what you don't like when you look in the mirror. Your own perception of yourself is much more important than what other people think of you. Yet another great saying: "What other people think of me is none of my business." If you walk around feeling good about yourself, then other people will pick up on that and perceive you as confident. Once you get in touch with the reality that you are perfect in your own unique way, and that you are the best you possible, you will have all the self-esteem you could ever need.

Remember this: what works for one person may not work for you; just as what works for you may not be right for anyone else. And that is perfectly OK! You must trust yourself, your instinct, your inner knowing—that is the Universe talking to you, that is your Higher Power, God, whatever you want to call it. There is something out there taking care of you and every one of us. I wouldn't be here today if that was not the truth. The best gift I gave myself as a teen was discovering my spirituality. Realizing that the Universe guides me, God is in control, and my Higher Power has the wisdom I need was a huge release of responsibility for me. I no longer had to do life alone.

I learned to "let go and let God," and things began to unfold with ease. I didn't have to try hard at all to be "my perfect" when I learned to trust the Universe to guide me. Doors began to open, opportunities and experiences started to mold me, and I found peace. Through funding my spirituality, I began to find myself. My spiritual outlook is what guided me through those rough teenage years.

Being unique is what we look like on the outside and our beliefs on the inside. We each have our own opinions and we are all entitled to that individuality. Being opinionated, dressing the way you want, finding a spiritual path that works for you is all part of growing up. Take your teenage years as a learning experience. When things fall apart or don't go the way you want, it is not the end of the world; it is not how the rest of your life is going to unfold. These years are merely one tiny part of your entire life. Do not give it more power than it deserves. Just watch, in ten years that gorgeous, popular person that was so mean to you will have let themselves go; that hot guy or girl you are crushing on who does not give you a second glance will be begging you to date them. Guess what? In ten years, you will not even remember what that person said that made you cry or even think that guy or girl is good looking anymore. Why? Because you will have grown and changed. You will have embraced your unique external and internal beauty, and other people's opinions of you will no longer matter. All that will matter is how you feel about yourself and that you have a strong spiritual connection to God, your Higher Power. When that is what matters most, then nothing but positivity will come your way. This is a journey to find your unique self. No one else has the right to define you. With God, you have the power to be whatever you that you want to create. Find yourself, your true you, through embracing your unique qualities and quirks. Find YOUR perfect!

I AM!

Angie Topbas, MBA CHHC

Angie Topbas, Certified Holistic Health Coach and American Association of Drugless Practitioners member, inspires families who aspire to lead a healthier and happier life. Angie is a mom and a graduate of the Institute for Integrative Nutrition. She received her MBA from Thunderbird in 2001, and she has a BA in Business Administration.

Angie, through her individual and group health coaching programs, supports families around setting and measuring health and lifestyle goals, teaches how to make healthier choices at grocery stores and restaurants, and guides on preparing quick and easy, healthy but tasty meals and snacks for the whole family.

🏠 http://www.lusciousnutritious.com

🏠 http://www.balanceforbusymoms.com

✉ angie@lusciousnutritious.com

✉ angie.topbas@gmail.com

I AM!

f www.facebook.com/lusciousnutritious

f www.facebook.com/AngieTopbas

in Angie (Enci) Topbas

🐦 www.twitter.com/AngieTopbas

📷 Instagram: @AngieTopbas

Ⓢ Skype: encitopbas75

📞 212-300-5785

CHAPTER 17

I Am Balanced

By Angie Topbas, MBA CHHC

I close my eyes as I try to fall asleep, thinking that I will be turning thirty-nine this summer. Suddenly, I find myself talking to my teenage self. "Whatever you do for yourself, for your parents, or for others, you will never be perfect. You are already perfect the way you are." "Please let go of this perfectionism—it will bring you more harm than good." "Stop starving yourself with fad diets. Try to find out what works and what does not work for your body, mind, and spirit." "You will regret being a couch potato in front of the TV. Just get up, go out for a walk, or find a physical activity that you will enjoy…"

Growing up, I was the neat and organized one, trying to be perfect all the time. I remember the times when my parents' friends asked me whether I would want a brother or a sister. Every time this question was asked, I said no. A sibling would mess up my room and keep me from my homework. My organized life had to stay the way it was, and nobody had the right to ruin my routine. As a result, I stayed the only child.

I had always been a very hardworking student and graduated at the top my class. My parents were lucky; they never had to put pressure on me to study because if I didn't get a chapter right, I would repeat, repeat, and repeat to make sure I learned it perfectly. Although I had a relatively happy childhood, being the way I was, I missed out on wonderful feelings. I didn't play any sports, other than my weekly ice-skating with my best friend; I didn't participate in any extra-curricular activities; I didn't spend much time in nature. When I was a teenager, if I knew what I know now, I would have lived those years to the fullest and perhaps would not have suffered from acid reflux/gastritis, anxiety and panic attacks, and severe migraines.

My perfectionism continued throughout my college years. Only after I turned thirty, got married, and had a baby, I realized that all areas of my life could not be perfect all the time and that is perfectly normal. Especially when I had a baby at home, I had to prioritize things—for example, if my baby was hungry and my house was unorganized, what would I choose to do? Feed my baby or organize? Of course, feed the baby first. Similarly, when my toddler was running around, would I follow her so she wouldn't hurt herself or empty the dishwasher? Of course, the answer was to follow her.

I encourage you to take a closer look at different areas of your life: school and grades, involvement in sports or any other physical activity, relationships with your friends, teachers, and family, and religious or any other spiritual practices. Analyze each of these areas and find out if anything is out of balance. For me, the importance of my grades made me perfect in that area, but I did not know that I was missing out a lot in other areas of my life. I wish I had a mentor to help me realize that school was not my whole life and that if I got a B or C in an exam, I would still be OK.

Having balance in different areas of your life is essential to become a healthy and happy individual. You might think about balance in two categories—physical and emotional. Physical balance can be achieved through a healthier and more active body. Emotional balance can be attained through self-love, healthy relationships, spirituality, etc. There are several chapters in this book shedding light on how to attain emotional balance. So, as a Certified Holistic Health Coach, I felt responsible to take you through the steps towards physical balance.

Paying attention to what you eat and drink is key toward a healthier body and a healthier mind. As the founder of the Institute for Integrative Nutrition (IIN), Joshua Rosenthal says: "There is a strong correlation between food and mood. What you eat and drink affects the way you feel and the way you think." Different foods affect each of you in different ways. Pay attention to how you feel both physically and psychologically right after you eat a certain food, and again two hours after. Do you recognize any mood changes? Feeling bloated, heavy, lightheaded, happy, upset, and anxious? It might be hard to believe, but all those feelings could be due to a certain type of food. It took almost twenty years for me to figure out that my digestive issues were related to processed dairy and gluten, my panic attacks were triggered by too many cookies and cakes, and my migraines were aggravated by yin and yang imbalance and dehydration. Unfortunately, too many food-like (unnatural) substances surround us. Therefore, although feeding your body healthy and nutritious foods is easy, it can be challenging in this environment. Keep in mind this saying while grocery shopping: "If your grandmother can't recognize it, don't purchase it." Also, start by eating mindfully (without any disturbances like TV, so you can concentrate on what you are eating, how much you are eating, and when to stop), drinking plenty of water, replacing sugary sodas with fresh fruit or vegetable juices, switching to whole grains, using natural sweeteners, and trying to understand what works and what does not work for your body.

I was raised in a culture where there was too little emphasis on exercise. As a teenager, the circumference of my thighs started bothering me. I remember putting myself on severe diets, doing side-leg raises and applying cellulite creams in hope of losing the fat around my thighs and looking like my girlfriends that were skinny. However, I was a bit lazy in terms of physical exercise. During my teen years, my exercise involved nothing other than light stretching and dancing at home, and ice-skating once a week. After coming to the US for graduate school, I gained weight due to bigger portions and unhealthy foods. I did not like looking at myself in the mirror. My old clothes did not fit. I was determined to lose the weight. For a while, I was really hard on myself.

I started going to the gym at school and I eliminated junk foods. I tried yoga, aqua gymnastics, and light running. Then, when my daughter turned three years old, I started studying holistic health and nutrition at IIN in New York City, and exercise became part of my lifestyle. Exercise makes me feel better physically and psychologically, allowing for more energy throughout the day; and, I realize the importance of building muscles. These days, I do a mix of strength training and some sort of cardio, like jumping on the trampoline, running, or taking a Zumba class. If you are not into exercise, I encourage you to search for the type of movement that brings you happiness and joy. Not all of you would like playing basketball or enjoy running. It is still OK to expose yourself to different activities and find out the best type of movement for your mind, body, and spirit.

My mom tells me that forty years ago, you would not hear somebody saying, "I am under too much stress" or "I am stressed-out," yet most people I work with come to me with stress-related problems and illnesses. I would like to provide you with three easy yet effective stress management practices:

1. Laughter is one of the best remedies to release stress, as it activates the feel-good hormones in your body. So, laugh until your belly hurts and then laugh a little more.

2. Breathing helps to decrease stress, anxiety, and depression. Dr. Andrew Weil's 4-7-8 breathing technique helps me fall asleep within minutes when I need it in bed. Place the tip of your tongue against the ridge of tissue just behind your upper front teeth and keep it there through the entire exercise. Exhale completely through your mouth; inhale through your nose to a count of four; hold your breath to a count of seven; exhale completely through your mouth to a count of eight. Repeat this cycle three more times.

3. Lack of sleep can stress your body more than anything else you do. So, try to get at least eight hours of sleep each night. I can clearly see the difference of a good night's sleep even in my seven-year-old daughter. Whenever she sleeps eleven or twelve hours, she wakes up with an active brain, talking very intelligently for her age, and happy and in a good mood all day long. Isn't that what we all strive for?

It is built within each of you to live a healthy, happy, and balanced life. Get started today by telling yourself:

I listen with love to my body's messages.

I choose to be healthy and free.

Suzanne M. Gabli

Suzanne Gabli is a visionary whose strengths are in relationships and leadership. Suzanne is a bestselling internationally published author who writes about vision, overcoming adversity, her awakening to advocate for strong early childhood education, and, through her personal journey of reflection, that anything is possible.

Suzanne is owner and executive director of Building Blocks Preschool, An Early Childhood Learning Community—a nature-based school in Highland, Michigan. In this role, she has been published on the connection between the child and the Reggio Emilia approach to learning.

Suzanne has also excelled in the field of print and marketing since 1991 as a marketing strategist.

✉ suzannegabli@gmail.com

⌂ www.BuildingBlocksSchool.com

⌂ www.DBSPrintMarketing.com

𝐟 www.facebook.com/suzanne.gabli

I AM!

www.twitter.com/suzannegabli1

www.linkedin.com/in/suzannegabli/

CHAPTER 18

I Am Light

By Suzanne M. Gabli

Life is messy. I come from a messy childhood. I had a desperate need to be accepted, encouraged, understood, and loved. Can you identify? Did you want the same?

I have survived adversity. My parents wanted the American dream: one had an entrepreneurial risk-taking spirit, while the other sought the consistency of a paycheck and benefits. They battled addiction, depression, financial stress, and a failed marriage—but shared strong faith and love of family.

Our home was equal parts love and turmoil, fraught with financial insecurity. Dad, a real-estate broker, was always waiting on a check. Food would become scarce, and we would lose light until that check came in. At five, I learned to search closets and coat pockets for spare change.

Dad checked out. As sole provider, Mom's strong work ethic and drive strove to make things better for us kids. They first separated when I was ten and divorced when I was fifteen. Though relieved the two people I loved most were no longer hurting each other, that five-year period starting in middle school was the first time I felt deprived. I went to three different schools during fifth grade—lonely, ridiculed, and judged because I didn't have the right clothes, had braces on my buck front teeth, and was tall for my age. I just felt awkward.

We lived on a large property where I often played with my sister and brother. In my imagination, I could escape the realities of life. Play is a wonderful expression of freedom—outside climbing trees, walking, gardening, and painting. It was nature's environment that encouraged me to visualize a world that was beautiful, where I was beautiful and free to be me. With the sun on my face and wind in my hair, I felt peace, joy, and belonging. I could dream.

Very important to me were my talks with God, when I could try to process what was happening around me, asking, "Why is this happening to me?" Thus, processing my hurts and disappointments, I came to realize that I could do and be anything I wanted—I just had to believe in myself. The answers I sought were inside me. I could build a different kind of life if I could learn how to start the journey.

The first step was to overcome the fear that I would let people down if I was not perfect. Illusive perfection! We all know that no one is perfect, so why do we expect it of ourselves? I was so afraid to disappoint. Adversity had created in me a strong drive for success and ensuing fear of failure. Guilt, obligation, an overwhelming sense of responsibility, and the need to appear nice and kind turned me into the ultimate people pleaser.

I learned to create income at a young age—cutting lawns, weeding gardens, delivering newspapers, babysitting, and shoveling snow. Each experience taught me about boundaries, negotiation, effort, quality work, communication, and follow-through. I learned that hard work brings the gifts of confidence, abundance, relationship, commitment, tenacity, and belief in me.

But you can't please yourself and everyone else. Just as I had to stand up for myself with those childhood bullies, I continued to try to find my voice. Being the good girl and dealing with that little negative voice is something I still struggle with, but we are all responsible for our own creations, however they turn out.

I was fifteen, tall, and not wanting to draw attention to myself when the aunt with whom I had been so close talked about my changing adolescent body in front of my entire family. The hurt would haunt me for a very long time. She followed this with other chaotic episodes during which my father did not defend me. As badly as it hurt, I disengaged from these two unhealthy relationships. It was not easy and took a lot of courage.

I entered a committed relationship at twenty-three to a sweet guy who seemed to have it all together. I thought this would be the answer. Unfortunately, I found that he had serious addiction issues and that his loving and supportive family were his enablers. I had no choice but to walk away. I started then to lead with my head (intellect) and not my emotions, protecting my heart so I would not be hurt again.

Though maintaining my optimism and sunny outlook, I was still struggling with the scars of parental dysfunction, adult abuse of power, and bullying. I felt ready to relinquish the victim role but was still looking for answers in the wrong places.

I knew that forgiveness is a gift you give yourself, and that I no longer desired to harbor bitterness and hate. I had to forgive and hoped I could find a way to do so. I recognized that attitude is everything, and only by letting go and forgiving, could I overcome. I call it true grit.

A strong believer in lifelong learning and personal development, I started reading books that would inspire and motivate, surrounded myself with loving friends and family, and eventually married. My husband had a renovation, business and I worked as a marketing project manager. Eighteen months after the birth of our second child, my husband and I began our journey in early childhood education. During that time, God surprised us with baby number three.

It was through this journey that I found my awakening. We purchased a pre-school on several acres of land in order to offer quality early childhood education that is heart-centered. It was exciting to share my passion that every child deserves to be loved, understood, and given every opportunity during those first five formative years. I wanted to be the light—to offer children a taste of what I found as a child in nature's setting; to provide a natural, holistic, creative, inquiry-based, nurturing learning environment. Allowing the child to feel the joy of learning and to be respected for who they are. Creating by doing is a uniquely powerful way to learn.

When the 2008 recession hit, my husband's business folded, causing tough financial times for our family and fledgling school. It was a challenge that would test my faith, passion, and marriage. I focused on my relationship with Jesus—my Savior, Light, and the One whose love has always carried me. And I met an amazing life coach who encouraged me to finally let God take the lead.

I learned how to win the battle in my mind by entertaining no negative thoughts and strove to become a positive influence on myself and others. I learned that only your heart knows what is right and best for you and spent reflective time learning who I really am—my strengths, my love language, and how I best learn. I actively practice self-love and celebrate the good, leaving life's trials for God to handle for me.

I wanted better for myself and my family. I read. I talked to God—a lot. I learned that thoughts are very powerful, whether positive or negative—and that either is a choice. I practice gratitude, starting each morning thinking about all I'm thankful for, saying to myself, "I am so happy," and "These are the best days of my life." And they are, as each morning I ask the Holy Spirit to bless and guide my day.

My journey brought me back from my head to my heart. No longer numb, I want my heart to feel, despite the fact that means that sometimes it will feel pain. I have no regrets about the past, for it helped make me who I am today—and I like who I am today.

It is still hard for me to be the center of attention; the spotlight is very uncomfortable. But it is only in that spotlight that I can be a light to others—to share my pain and recovery, experience, and hope. I trust that God has a bigger plan for each of us, and that when we are heart-centered, we find the fuel to fire up our passion—to find our awakening.

It's that plan I seek now, rather than worrying about ego or being the good-girl people-pleaser. Chaos is as inevitable as it is unpleasant. But my experience is that it pushed me toward where I need to be. So I will share my story of adversity and overcoming and carry my torch and be a light to others.

I am proof to those who are still hurting that we can not only survive but thrive. This message is one of hope. Practice self-love and love others with an open heart. Forgive. Set healthy boundaries in your relationships, and when in doubt, trust your instincts. Align with joy; surround yourself with people who uplift you. Believe that anything is possible.

And step outside your comfort zone and be someone's light.

Warren Broad, CCHT MFT HAC

Warren Broad is a clinical hypnotherapist, life coach, and addictions specialist. Also a now-retired fireman. Warren began his counseling career as a group home worker, working with displaced youth and foster children. Warren's education is extensive, holding multiple diplomas in adult psychology, clinical hypnosis, an honors diploma in addictions counseling, and is a certified coach. Warren continues to add to his education annually. Warren is also the creator of the Recovery In The Now Program™, a coaching and support program for those suffering with addictions and compulsions.

Warren lives two hours north of Toronto, Ontario, Canada, with his wife, son, and three rescued dogs. From there, Warren runs his in-person and online coaching and counseling practice. Warren is also often found on the tennis court and volunteering in many local organizations. Warren's passion for helping individuals through their challenges is endless.

✉ hello@warrenrbroad.com

⌂ www.warrenrbroad.com

I AM!

www.facebook.com/pages/Warren-Broad-The-Recovery-Now-Life-Coach/140846495989334?fref=ts

www.linkedin.com/profile/view?id=59487653&trk

CHAPTER 19

I Am Positivity

By Warren Broad, CCHT MFT HAC

One thing I have learned over the years is that there is always an internal voice speaking to you. It speaks to you nonstop. It is forever present—sometimes in a positive manner, other times not.

What the voice is saying depends on your self-esteem. When you hear more encouraging words, your self-esteem is positive, and when your internal voice is telling you something cannot be done and you are not worth it, your self-esteem will suffer.

I know what it feels like when the voice speaks negatively to you, for that is what I heard for much of my childhood. My family life was a challenging one, to say the least. My brother committed suicide when I was just eight years old. After that, there were many incidents that contributed to stress in our home and they fed the negative talk I was hearing in my head.

In an environment of constant challenges, it was tough for good thoughts to fight for space, and they often ended up being crowded out by the bad ones. Over time, that negative voice gets drilled into your consciousness over and over and it becomes part of your identity. Deep down you know it is unnatural, but it takes a lot of energy to fight it and many times I did not have that kind of energy.

So what ends up happening is you try and come up with ways to cope. Some people channel their energies into one aspect of their life, such as school, sports, or work. Many others choose to escape through drugs and alcohol. I know that because I was one of those people.

It started out simply enough. Drugs made me feel better and it quieted the negative voice and eased my depression. My mood improved and I enjoyed myself more. I partied more often because I wanted to keep that voice quiet. Over time, it took more to keep the bad thoughts at bay, so I went deeper and used more often.

The negative voice grew stronger and depression routed itself deep within my core thoughts. The first step in my recovery journey was a traditional thirty-day outpatient program. I took some good things from that experience, and my abstinence lasted a short while.

Over the next few years, I lapsed in and out of addiction many times. I would start out fighting against the negative voice, but the depressive mind ultimately won the bulk of the time.

But within me, there was another voice, a voice that wanted things to get better and wanted to live in greater peace and happiness. But I was still battling, and at the end of my twenties, a couple years after my mother's death, I had a nervous breakdown. Fighting the negative voice was tiring, and I could not take it any longer. I felt as if my spirit was dead, that I was a shell of a human being. It was at the point I knew my long-term physical and mental health were at stake. In the times where I lost hope, I considered suicide.

Something inside of me kept me going. I began reading self-help books and books on spirituality and meditation. I also found a gifted coach who created an environment in which I was free to talk. Over time, I began to understand and recognize that the internal voice was separate from me.

Once I learned that negative talk did not define me, and that I was truly "not my mind," I was on the road to recovery. I probed what fed the negative voice. I became aware that I was not living in the present. I was consistently living in the past. I also began to reframe the traumas of my childhood into empowering dialogue and beliefs, so that they could no longer be used against me.

Everyone has a voice speaking to them. It can be positive, negative, or both. Unfortunately, the major influences in my formative years created a lot of negative thoughts, feelings, and dialogue. Over time, I started to strengthen the internal positive voice. Like a muscle that had not been used for a while, I had to practice, and it felt foreign to me. Eventually, with the help of a trusted counselor, and thanks to healthy relationships with close friends, and my ever-supportive wife, I was able to change that voice to one that was much more positive.

The changes were remarkable. Before, when I was sad, my negative voice focused my attention on all of the loss and difficulties of my childhood. I would obsess on feeling robbed and deprived of a functional and happy childhood. My mind would remain rooted in the past. I would spend my days with the bulk of my thinking there and completely ignore the present. I would stay in the "poor me" mindset for days at a time. I was in a cognitive funk that focused on loss and misery. But one night, at 2 a.m., looking out into the forest, I had transformative moment. I let myself see that I would not be who I am without all those occurrences having happened. All that struggle and all that pain produced an incredibly empathic, caring individual. I decided in that moment that anytime my mind was in the negative or in the past, I would be thankful and grateful. I would actively redirect every time I noticed the negative occurring.

Being human, I still make mistakes, and on days when I feel less energetic and positive, the negative voice does still want to creep in at times. But with cognitive awareness (being aware of what we think), I can catch that voice early on and implement what is needed to move that voice back to a positive space. You see, our minds are like iPods on repeat. If the iPod is left alone on repeat without installing new music, it will simply play the same songs over and over again endlessly until we install something new.

This was one of the most important realizations I ever had after recognizing that I was not just my internal dialogue. Whether you are religious, spiritual, or neither, we can all use positive affirmations to begin installing new internal dialogue. All scripture is in many ways a long list of positive affirmations based around various illustrative stories. Our access in the Internet and electronic age is larger than it has ever been for finding resources for positive affirmations and positive reinforcement.

I also choose to focus my social time on developing healthy relationships with healthy people. Whether you are an introvert or extrovert, we can all make use of and benefit from surrounding ourselves with those people in our lives that are positive rather than negative. We can all build each other up, share positive experiences, and enjoy sharing a positive space together.

In life, no amount of advice can help you as much as things you have no choice but to endure. What was once a big unfamiliar situation with an endless number of possibilities becomes something that you can survive and even direct, because you have that experience and that confidence.

When I was younger, most of my experience was negative, and this is what fed that negative voice. When I felt sad or stressed, the default position my mind went to was negative, but now that I regularly install new positive dialogue, I have become an optimist! That is something I would have never said was possible fifteen years ago. It was not even within a frame of reference at that time. Now that I have survived that period and am thriving, I have a growing body of positive experiences and affirmations that I can rely on to remind myself that, while yes, there will always be challenges, there is also plenty of good, and that what I focus most on, I get more of. Life for me now is creative. It is not out of my control. I do not need to wait to see what my mind decides on. I get to decide, and what a wonderful thing that is!

I encourage you all to evaluate your mental dialogue and assess if it is working in your favor. If you see that it isn't, never accept it and know that it is changeable. You can be the controller of your mind and your life. You never need to accept the default your mind or your circumstances have created to this point.

Enjoy this positive affirmation as a start to your new way of thinking.

"I will think positively and embrace the good in my life."

Thank you. Warren Broad, CCHT

Evelyn "The Heart Lady" Polk, LMFT

Evelyn is a licensed Marriage, Family, and Child therapist in Vallejo, CA, where she is Owner/Clinical Supervisor of "Talk To M.E." Counseling, Founder/Director of For a Child's H.E.A.R.T., Inc., and Member of the Les Brown Platinum Speakers Network.

She is author of four books and is also Producer/Host of the Public Access television talk show, *Visions For A Child's Heart*, and Internet radio talk show, *HEART Talk with Ms. E*, both dedicated to nurturing those whose lives are impacted by foster care and adoption and other life challenges.

Her most valued role, however, is that of foster/adoptive parent and mentor to her many "babies" over the past three decades.

Connect with Ms. E:

⌂ www.TalkToMsE.com

🐦 www.Twitter.com/TweetheartLady

I AM!

f **Talk to ME/Let ME Speak: Ms. Evelyn The Heart Lady (On Facebook)**

🎙 **www.blogtalkradio.com/hearttalkwithmse**

▶ **www.youtube.com/user/MsEHeartLady**

🏠 **www.ForAChildsHeart.org**

🏠 **www.HEARTTalkPublications.com**

CHAPTER 20

I Am Loved

By Evelyn "The Heart Lady" Polk

Over the past thirty-plus years I have worked as a residential counselor, social worker, and therapist, as well as taken tremendous joy (along with some pain) in being a foster/adoptive parent and mentor. One of the greatest gifts I've received in all of my experiences is watching young people (and old alike) respond to the sense of being loved, and being loved by them in return.

My youngest son was about six years old when one day I was cutting his hair and he just would not be still! He kept twisting and turning his head, looking up at me smiling with his little snaggletooth self. I asked him why he kept looking at me, and he said "When you touch me like that, it makes my heart warm." Then he added, "And it's never felt like that before."

That moment became a defining point in my life. Although I'd always loved the children and youth I came into contact with, I then knew without a shadow of doubt that my life purpose was to make a child's heart warm. Shortly thereafter, when I started my non-profit organization for foster/adoptive youth, I determined that the mission, and every aspect of services provided, would also be to make a child's heart warm. I named it "For a Child's H.E.A.R.T."

I've counseled many youth who have been brought to me to be "treated" for "mental health issues" because of their "acting out" behaviors. For the majority of these young people, I've found that most of their "issues" have really been emotional ones stemming from matters of the heart. Feelings of having been abandoned, rejected, unheard, misunderstood, confused, and unloved—all of which are underlying factors of anger.

Perhaps you may know what it feels like to have been separated from your biological family—whether at birth or during later childhood—and even further, numerous other separations of being bounced from home to home through the foster care system, and even disrupted adoptive placements.

You may not have had this particular experience, but most of us have experienced the loss of someone and/or something we've been attached to, whether due to relocation, divorce, or even death. When we experience these losses, we may question: "Why does everyone I love leave me?" "Why do these things keep happening to me?" "What's wrong with me?" I believe we all desire to have a place to call "home" and someone who will always be there for us, to love us unconditionally. Such losses can leave us with a feeling of being punished and unloved.

The first major and core loss of my life was that of my father, which occurred in two phases. The first phase occurred before I was school age, at the time of his and my mother's marital separation. Being a "Daddy's Girl," I was saddened not to have my daddy to prepare and share breakfast with me before being taken to my godparents when he'd leave for work on the mornings before my mother returned home from her night shifts at the hospital. I missed jumping into his arms when he returned from work later in the day and finding a bag of Cheetos or some other treat in his lunch pail, which he stopped at the store to buy for me on the way home.

I eventually adapted to my parents' separation, and I even became grateful as I became older, to be able to have time away from my mother during weekend visits with my father. I sometimes felt that my mother minimized the love I felt in my relationship with my father because he was no longer there fulltime. However, I never doubted his love for me and I always knew I was his "baby."

The final phase of losing my dad occurred when I was fourteen years old, when he died.

That was totally unexpected! I was not prepared to be picked up from school in the middle of the school day by a neighbor and arrive home to learn that my father had died in his sleep. His body had been discovered when he didn't show up for work that day. The days which followed were a blur and seemed almost surreal. Everyone made sure to keep me "busy" during the funeral preparation, and following that, I immediately returned to school.

Although my father was gone and I missed him sorely, I wasn't left feeling completely "fatherless," as I still had my godfather—who had been in my life since infancy, my younger sister's father who treated me as if I was his own, and the father of my new best friend, who happened to be born on my father's birthday. They did a wonderful job of creating a hedge of caring and protection around me throughout my high school and college years. However, it wasn't the same as being able to curl up into Daddy's lap and lay my head against his chest.

When I was in my mid-twenties, both my godfather and my friend's father died within months of one another. Since I referred to both of them as my godfathers, when I took off work to attend the second funeral, a co-worker asked me if my godfather had nine lives.

The accumulation of paternal figure losses impacted my life more than I initially realized. It was not long after that when I began to experience unexplainable bouts of depression which seemed to deepen with time.

One day, at the beginning of a therapy session, which happened to be held in the home of my therapist because she was experiencing back problems and needed to remain in a supine position on her couch—talk about switching seats—she said, "Tell me about your father..." and that's "all she wrote" that day. She'd turned on the water faucet, and I sobbed buckets of tears from the pit of my belly, for practically the whole one-hour session...tears which had been accumulating and bottled up for over fifteen years! Bottom line...I didn't feel ANYONE loved me like my father had, and he had left me! I'd been wanting someone to love me unconditionally as my father had, and I also wanted to be able to love a child as my father had loved me, and that hadn't happened.

Fast forward another ten years or so, after a long-term relationship and an engagement had ended, my son had run away from home, and it seemed like everyone and everything had been taken from me. I felt like I was being punished! My then-pastor stepped up to the podium one Sunday and said to the congregation: "I want you to just take this time of worship to crawl up into the lap of Jesus and bury your head in his breast and just let Him love you." Yep, there came another hour of bucket-filled tears. From childhood, I'd learned the Sunday school and vacation Bible songs "Yes, Jesus Loves Me," and "Oh, How He Loves You and Me," but it had never felt it as "up close and personal" as it did then.

It just also happens that the pastor's father actually became a surrogate father to me, and he came the closest to making me feel loved the way I did with my father, more than anyone had. I didn't get up in his lap but I'd run into his arms and he'd give me the biggest and most assuring bear hugs!

As the years have passed, I have still have my share of days of feeling alone, but I know without a shadow of doubt that I am loved by "Thee Father," the One who created me and laid out a plan and purpose for my life. There are times when things have happened so suddenly and unexpectedly that I've excitedly jumped up and down and squealed with the delight of a child, "God REALLY does love me!"

If you're like me, you may be thinking, "Yeah, but I need to feel some love with a physical body." I recently had an epiphany of the manifestation of the love embodied in the answer to a prayer I prayed as a child—for a little sister. My sister, Kim, whom I refer to as "the Angel," was born with Down Syndrome when I was eleven years old. I am now her primary caregiver, and it occurred to me that the love I receive from her, and in caring for her, is probably the greatest embodiment of unconditional love one could experience on this earth! I am reminded of my favorite quotes:

"To the world, you may be only one person, but to one person you may be the world"
—Author Unknown

She constantly reminds me that I am her world, and I consider myself highly favored to be the recipient and custodian of such a precious treasure as her being; as well as all of the children and youth whose lives I'm privileged to be a part of.

I believe when we're able to see and recognize "the big picture" and receive the God-given gift of love for and of ourselves from "Our Daddy," then give lovingly and freely to others, it gravitates to us from places we may least expect it, and our hearts are fulfilled. I know I am loved and so are YOU.

When you feel it least, say out loud and repeat it over and over until you feel it in your heart of hearts: **"I am loved."**

I AM!

Tim Eastman

Tim Eastman is a physical education teacher at First Baptist Christian School in Grand Cayman. He completed his undergraduate studies at Central Michigan University and is currently working on completing his master's degree in physical education pedagogy from Western Michigan University. Before teaching in Grand Cayman, he taught K-8 physical education and health at Hope of Detroit Academy in Detroit, Michigan. Prior to teaching, he was working in professional baseball as an umpire, but he realized there was a different purpose for his life. He enjoys spending time with his wife and son, attending church, working out, time with family, and watching/playing sports.

Tim Eastman Contact Information:

✉ timothymeastman@gmail.com

f https://www.facebook.com/pages/Tim-Eastman/1411080939144720?ref=br_tf

CHAPTER 21

I Am Forgiven

By Tim Eastman

"It can't happen to me, Bob!" is a response that I gave when I was in the "No Sex Club" in high school. I played the character Nick in a game show, and Nick didn't think *he* could contract a sexually transmitted disease/infection (STD/STI). His answer to everything was "It can't happen to me!" In high school, I played Nick, but in college I became "Nick."

In high school, I was involved in many activities—hockey and baseball, school sporting events and dances, student council, homecoming float construction, etc. I lost my virginity my senior year of high school while intoxicated on spring break in Cancun, Mexico.

I stayed home my first year of college and attended Mott Community College in Flint, Michigan, because I felt that I was not ready to go away to school. My second year of college, I attended Central Michigan University (CMU) in Mt. Pleasant, Michigan. I partied excessively in college and was very sexually active. A majority of my sexual activity happened after consuming alcohol. Alcohol negatively affected my judgment and ultimately led to poor decision-making. While at CMU, I remember being in one of my methods classes and each of us had to teach a lesson in our major. A girl taught a lesson on sex education and did an activity where we had to pick a piece of paper out of a bag. After everyone picked a piece of paper out of the bag, she told us what the colors meant. I don't remember the color that I had; however, whatever color I had meant that I passed an STI to different people in the class. I froze; it seemed like time just stopped! I had a pit in my stomach. I was in denial...IT CAN'T HAPPEN TO ME! I already had an STI before this point—Chlamydia—but drinking an antibiotic cured it. I remember sitting in the clinic and filling out a questionnaire. In the questionnaire, it asked: "How many partners have you had?" I lied and put a different number because I was embarrassed and didn't want the nurse to know. I not only lied to the nurse, but I lied to partners that I had sex with. If they asked how many girls I had slept with, I gave them a low-ball answer so that they would have sex with me. Despite having contracted an STI, I continued to think: "It couldn't happen to me, not again! However, it could, and yes, it did happen again.

The STI that I currently have is the most common according to the Center for Disease Control and it is called the human papillomavirus (HPV). According to the CDC, about 79 million Americans are currently infected with HPV. I did not have any visual signs or symptoms of HPV, which is common for both men and women. I found out that I had it when a girl that I was dating contracted genital warts. What a terrible feeling! Do you think that stopped me? I wish, but no it didn't. I knew from reading different things that most people with HPV do not show signs or symptoms, so I continued to be sexually active. I took advantage of these girls, knowing full well that I had an STI and put them at risk for potential health problems that can come from HPV, such as genital warts and cervical cancer. If a particular girl called me that I had relations with, I would hesitate to answer because I thought they would tell me that they contracted genital warts and would be mad at me.

The negative consequences of my sexual behavior did not end there though. While in college, I got a phone call from a girl that I had past relations with and she said with a trembling voice, "Tim, I am pregnant!" My heart sunk as if I was on a roller coaster going downhill at 100 mph. We decided that we were not "ready" to be parents and that we had hopes and dreams ahead of us. We decided that we were going to abort the child, so we went to a clinic. Here, we found out that she actually was not pregnant. We were relieved.

After I graduated from college, I went on to work in professional baseball as an umpire. We worked mainly at night, which left most of the day free. A typical day while working in baseball would be: get up around 10:00 a.m., eat breakfast, workout, eat lunch, be back at the hotel by 1:30 p.m., surf the Internet, take a nap from 3:00-4:30 p.m., shower, get ready, and leave for the ballpark around 5:30 p.m. for a 7:00 p.m. game. For me, I found this free time to be very dangerous. While surfing the web, I became addicted to pornography. Pornography really messes with your head and gives you a severely jaded mindset on how one should perform and act during sex. I saw how the men treated the women and that is how I thought I was supposed to act. Pornography affected my relationship with my wife, Nicole, when we first started dating—that, in addition to the baggage that I had from past relationships. I told her upfront that I had HPV, and thankfully, she had the Gardasil shot when she was younger. After Nicole and I were married, she diagnosed me with attention deficit hyperactivity disorder (ADHD) and narcolepsy, which was confirmed by other physicians. Thankfully, I married a doctor! A trait of ADHD is being impulsive. This does not go well with alcohol, which lowers your inhibition. I guess I was addicted to sex. Every time I had sex, I just wanted more. I was searching for love and acceptance from others in all the wrong places. The more sex I had, the more I wanted sex, and the more I had sex, the emptier and more deflated I became. I felt like a scumbag. I was lost and broken.

I hurt many people with my selfish actions. My emotions are stirring right now as I write this. I am embarrassed and ashamed of my actions that have caused people both physical and psychological harm. I am writing this chapter so that someone will learn from all of the pain that I have caused others, and of the guilt, fear, regret, and anger that I have experienced.

Learn from my experiences and know that it is wise to wait to have sex. Sex is supposed to be special between a man and a woman; what a wonderful and beautiful bond that you can share with your spouse. I know that so often you hear of sex being related to the car analogy, "Drive it before you buy it." However, I'd like you to take another look at this with new insight, so take a moment to really think about a used and new car. With a used car, you could be unaware of how many owners had possession over it, how many accidents broke it down and left it in need of repair, or what ongoing problems the car will have because of past incidents. Even if it looks "perfect" from the outside, you do not necessarily know the history that lies beneath, right? In comparison, there is something beautiful about that new car, knowing that you are the first to touch it, to feel it, and to belong with it. There is no unnecessary baggage weighing that new relationship down and the journey is smoother.

I have lived with so much guilt, anger, regret, and frustration; and, it was not until I gained a relationship with Jesus Christ that I learned that I am forgiven! I have repented, and I realize that it is not through my deeds, but through the act of Christ, that my sins are forgiven, and that gives me hope and healing.

If you have engaged in premarital sex, it is not too late to abstain until you're married. If you feel the temptation to engage in sex, then I urge you to reconsider and to realize that yes, it can happen to you. Here is my advice to you:

- Love yourself for you.

- Make a decision to abstain from sex and to avoid situations where you may fall to temptation.

- Try to abstain from alcohol.

- Find God. He is awesome and He will never forsake you.

- Find an accountability partner who is routed in faith. You two can talk to each other and discuss your challenges in life.

- Get into His word. I am not saying life is going to be easy if you are a believer; however, you may avoid some situations by reading the Bible.

In conclusion, my past does not define who I am today. Thankfully, I have a beautiful wife who accepts me despite my past; and, I believe that God put her into my life to make me a better person. Now, I strive to be a positive role model for our son, Jack. You can only hide your secrets for so long until they surface; and it is my hope that through sharing this with others, they will respect their body and the bodies of others.

I AM!

Ashley Love

Ashley Love is an author, poet, and entrepreneur, but her most rewarding role is mother. She is the single mother of three daughters who are four, six, and eight. She is the founder of her own personal/professional/artist development business, Charged Visions, and leads the phenomenal tribe #ElegantlyChargedVisionaries. In 2013, Ashley co-founded Poets Against Bullying, an organization of people who are tired of staying quiet and letting bullying and abuse destroy the lives of many children, as well as adults. Ashley's first poetry book, *Tainted Elegance: In the Key of Love,* is now available.

📞 **318-880-8215**

✉ **chargedvisions@gmail.com**

🏠 **www.chargedvisions.com**

ⓕ **www.facebook.com/writerashleyl**

ⓕ **www.facebook.com/chargedvisions**

ⓕ **www.facebook.com/poetsagainstbullying**

🐦 **www.twitter.com/writerashleyl**

CHAPTER 22

I Am Me

By Ashley Love

My voice is powerful. I can make a difference. My today will be better than my yesterday. Those are just a few of the phrases I repeat to myself in the mirror every morning as I get dressed, brush my teeth, and prepare myself for my day.

For most of my life, I battled with the mirror. I had issues with self-esteem and I had a hard time being comfortable in my own shoes. I yearned for other people's approval. I listened to what other people had to say and never stood my own ground for a fear of being judged. The mirror became my enemy, my own reflection tainted with imperfections. It all started when I was a child…

I was an introverted, shy-to-a-fault girl that made excellent grades in school and was most notably titled the "teacher's pet." I enjoyed school while many of those around me were only there because they had to be. I had a love for learning, and while other kids wanted Nintendo games and bikes for Christmas and their birthday, I wanted a journal and pens. From a young age, I used writing as a way to release the pent-up feelings that I had inside but couldn't verbally express. Being the "teacher's pet" wasn't an easy job. Because I would rather study or read, rather than hangout and have fun, I was bullied by the other kids. They made fun of me by calling me names, pinching me, taking my things, and pulling my hair. I was such a quiet child and I had no idea my worth. I let them get away with it. I didn't think I had it inside me to stand up for myself. The bullying crushed my spirits and self-worth even more, and although I was involved in many activities, and the teachers loved me, I was very unhappy.

In high school, I was in JROTC and won many honors for my schoolwork, as well as volunteer work. I was involved in many activities, but I was still a loner because I didn't believe in myself. After my sophomore year, my grandmother, mother, and I moved to another state. I was crushed because I had to leave the few real friends that I had behind and I had to go to a new school. My junior year was very difficult because I didn't know anyone at my new school and it was full of cliques. I made very few friends, so I spent most of my free time at school, writing. My peers didn't understand me and I became known there as "the book worm." One day, someone even stole my notebook with all of my poems and stories in it, and I never got it back. I was told at the end of my junior year that my credits would not transfer from the school I went to back home in New Orleans, LA. The classes had different names and they couldn't put them towards my credits to graduate. I was crushed when they told me that I would have to repeat my junior year just to make up for it. All I had accomplished with my effort was being taken from me. My mother pulled me out of school and I got my GED before the kids in my class graduated.

I yearned at seventeen for acceptance, mainly from a man. My parents divorced when I was eight, and I didn't get to spend much time with my father. I was a daddy's girl and that has affected me throughout not only my childhood but my adulthood as well. I had a misconstrued conception of what love was. I got into a serious relationship and got pregnant with my first daughter that year. I still went to a technical college and finished with a 3.97 grade-point average. I got in with the wrong crowd of so-called-friends that weren't motivated to go after their visions, and that led me to believe that making something of my life was just plain hopeless. I had my second daughter at twenty and my youngest daughter at twenty-two. During those years, I was still searching for a love for myself and some kind of fulfillment. I let other people run my life and that opened me up to mental and physical abuse. I felt I deserved being hurt and having my spirit torn down.

At twenty-three, I was a divorced, single mother of three young girls, and then I got some bad news: My grandmother was terminally ill, and my mother was diagnosed with colon cancer. I was working in the medical field and left my job so I could care for them. During that next year, things took a turn for the worst—I lost my grandmother who was my biggest motivator, and my mom, my kids, and I became homeless. We stayed in extended living until we were able to get an apartment. I lost hope in my life, and I knew I had to find what was missing. I always prayed, but I never trusted in God's plan. I always wanted to do things my way and ended up getting hurt or put myself in a bad situation.

I got down on my knees and prayed for God to take away my pain, replace the negative people in my life with positive people that would encourage me, and help me see the vision that He had for my life. I made a decision one day that I was going to change the direction my life was headed. It took a lot of praying and soul-searching, and many nights, I cried myself to sleep. I had to first learn to love myself. That mirror could no longer be a battlefield plagued by hate, but it had to be a reflection of love. It took years to finally be able to say, "I love myself, and although I may not be perfect, I am the perfect version of what God wants me to be."

When you don't have a love for yourself, you are more susceptible to bullying and abuse because your standards are not as high for people you allow into your life. You may put up with more because you are looking for acceptance in another person rather than looking at their character first. I am listing my five principles for building confidence and developing self-love below.

1. It all starts with your mindset. What you believe is the basis for the actions you take in your life. Create a mission statement for "you." Who are you and where do you want to go in life? Start reciting positive affirmations daily. Affirmations train your mind to think positively rather than negatively.

2. Destroy all of the negative "weeds" in your life, so that you can grow into the beautiful garden you desire to. Negative people and negative situations should no longer be allowed entrance into your life.

3. Create a plan for what you want to accomplish and list the steps you need to take to make each goal a reality. If there is something preventing you from loving yourself, change it. Make a list of all

COMPILED BY **NICOLE EASTMAN, D.O.**

the things that you would like to change about yourself, then write down ways you can change that perception.

4. Commit to each goal and then take action. A plan means nothing if there is no action.

5. Take time for yourself daily to learn who you are and get refocused for the next day. When you have that special "me" time, you are less likely to become overwhelmed by stressful situations and you stay connected to your inner being. Take charge of your life because you are the ONLY person who can.

I am now able to face that mirror image of my reflection without pain, hurt, guilt, and hate. I can now smile because I am in charge of my life, and God is in total control. I am beautiful. I am strong. I am a good woman. I am a loving mother. I am following God's vision for my life. I am worth it. I AM ME!

I have a free eBook called *Confidently Walk in Your Purpose and Create The #Progress You Desire*. Send an email to chargedvisions@gmail.com with "I AM ME" in the subject line to receive the eBook.

I AM!

Chris Musgrove

Chris Musgrove is a youth minister and evangelist whose main thrust of his twenty-nine years in youth ministry has been involved in motivating youth to get a vision for their lives. Chris founded "FutureNow," a School Assembly Outreach Program in April 2001. He and his family travel and minister all over the United States and have ministered in thirteen countries.

He is also author of "Daily Stir," a devotional that goes out to thousands every day.

Chris and his wife Terri currently reside in Valdosta, GA, and have four children and one son-in-law—Josh and Kasey (Musgrove) Burk, twenty-seven; Christian, twenty-four; Victoria, twenty; Isaac, fourteen; and twin grandbabies Jack and Lucy, two!

CHAPTER 23

I Am Vision

By Chris Musgrove

I was in seventh grade when I decided school was a waste of time. So I made up my mind that I was going to do just enough to get by. My report cards reflected this and always included messages like: creates a disturbance in class, poor study habits, and failure to follow directions.

Upon entering high school, because of my lack of vision and no care attitude, I would do anything for attention, which kept me in the principal's office. I was in ninth grade the first time I was offered to smoke pot, and I freely accepted. I was living for the now and could care less about my future. I had no vision, no purpose, and no plans.

I once heard someone say, "If you don't know where you're going, you'll take every road." **Proverbs 29:18** says, "Without a vision, my people perish." That was me—I didn't know where I was going and I didn't care. The only thing I accomplished in high school, other than barely graduating, was being voted "Class Clown."

After graduating from high school, I didn't know what I was going to do, and as I said before, I didn't really care. I had friends going to Florida State University in the fall, so I applied there and was accepted, even though my SAT score was below the required acceptance score.

Moving to a college town where drugs and alcohol were more accessible only compounded my problem. My first semester at Florida State, I made three F's and a D, my second semester I made three F's and an F. From high school to my first year in college, I had been arrested twice, had multiple wrecks with a few totaled vehicles, kicked out of school, driver's license revoked, no job, and still no vision or plan.

I have to admit, for the first time in my life, this class clown was depressed. I had no idea where I was going and it was taking me down every road but the right one. Someone close to me left me a Christian booklet in my apartment, and thankfully, I read it one night. In the booklet was a prayer to receive Jesus Christ and that night I called on Jesus. **Romans 10:13** says, "Whoever calls on the name of the Lord shall be saved."

I believed it was God's plan for me to get back in college and get my degree and finish what I started. Nobody in my family had ever graduated from college, and by God's grace, I was going to do it. To the glory of God, I got back into school and in 1983, I received my bachelor's degree from Florida State University.

I left Tallahassee, Florida, and moved to Broken Arrow, Oklahoma, to attend Rhema Bible College that same year. After graduating from Rhema in June of 1985, I moved back to Live Oak, Florida, and became youth pastor of Melody Christian Center. That same summer, I met my wife Terri, and we were married the next year.

In the spring of 1991, the local Fellowship of Christian Athlete's Area Director Steve McHargue asked me to help him facilitate a weeklong assembly program in several schools in four different counties in our area. That week, we were in five high schools and middle schools in five days, and at the end of the week on Friday night, we planned an evangelistic outreach and invited all the students to attend. To our surprise, over 2,200 students showed up and over four hundred prayed to receive Jesus.

Something else exciting happened that night; a vision was birthed in my heart. To experience seeing 2,200 students show up and with four hundred responding in a place like Live Oak let me know it could happen anywhere.

I caught myself sharing what happened that night with everyone I came in contact with. I believed that God had allowed me to see that to drop a vision in me. A vision is what keeps you awake at night—it's your passion, it's all you can think or talk about. **Matthew 12:34** says, "Out of the abundance of the heart the mouth speaks." The **New International Version** says, "For the mouth speaks what the heart is full of."

What I was doing by sharing my vision with everyone can be explained in the Bible. **Habakkuk 2:2-3** says, "Write the vision and make it plain on tablets, that he may run who reads it. For the vision is yet for an appointed time; but at the end it will speak, and it will not lie. Though it tarries, wait for it; because it will surely come, it will not tarry."

Seven years later in 1998, the vision started coming to pass while on a mission in Liverpool, England, with some students. While there, we were invited to do an assembly at a school that John Lennon attended. We asked the principal if it was all right to do a Christian program and he said yes.

At the close of the assembly, one student responded, and as he came forward to pray, the other students began laughing at him. It bothered me that they were laughing, so I yelled to get them to stop. I didn't know what I was going to say at that point, but thank God, the Holy Spirit did. Without even thinking, I said by the inspiration of the Holy Spirit, "They say John Lennon went to this school, and John Lennon said the Beatles would be more popular than Jesus Christ. But John Lennon is dead and in his grave, but Jesus Christ rose from His grave and He (Jesus) is what this young man has come to receive today." Amazingly, two-thirds of those students got out of their seats and made their way to the front of the stage.

What happened next is what kept me awake at night for months after that trip. April Perez, one of the young ladies on our mission team, told me after the assembly, "When we get back to Florida, we've got to do this!" I told her that what just happened was against the law in Florida, and she responded," Isn't there something we can do?" Her words rang in my head for many weeks after that, and all I could think about was the vision God had given me about going into the public schools.

Three years later in 2001, we did our first FutureNow public school assembly program in Florida, and although we couldn't share the gospel of Jesus Christ, we could share about vision. The name "FutureNow" came from **Jeremiah 29:11**, which says, "I know the plans I have for you declares the Lord, to give you a future and a hope."

A year later, we were invited to another school, and at the same time we were transitioning from youth pastors to Interim Pastors at

Lighthouse Christian Center in Mayo, FL. During our two years at the church, we did seven school assemblies. Because of the success of FutureNow, in the spring of 2004, we stepped down as pastors to pursue FutureNow fulltime.

Days before we stepped down, someone told me, "If you leave your job, your four children will starve to death." I wish you could see the students' faces, during an assembly, when I repeat that to them and then say, "The same people that told me that will tell you can't graduate, or go to college, or play football, or be a nurse, or open your own restaurant. People that don't have a vision are going to tell you that you can't have one."

Something else I share in the assemblies is the class clown thing was actually a gifting that I never developed. But I didn't allow the teachers to help me determine and then develop my gifts, because there was no application. I then like to say that a wise King once said, "A man's gift makes room for him and brings him before great men." (**Proverbs 18:16**). And my gift has brought me to this school today, and I am before greatness. Because there's greatness inside every one of you students and it is waiting to be let out. And drugs, alcohol, premarital sex, gangs, violence, failing grades, etc., aren't the problem; they're just symptoms of the real problem. You don't have a vision, but it can start today. Your future is now."

Once I allowed God into my life, the vision became clear. Allow God to show you the vision He has for you, to give you a future and a hope.

It has been ten years since I was told my four kids would starve if I quit my job. Since then, we have been in over 180 schools, seen one hundred eighty thousand students, with twenty thousand making commitments to Jesus Christ. My children didn't starve, and they are all in some way involved in FutureNow. Glory to God!

For more information on Chris Musgrove and FutureNow go to www.futurenow.us

I AM!

Hannah Brennan

Hannah Brennan is a twenty-one-year-old playwright and student from London. Her play, *Soap and Water*, was hailed as "one of the most daring pieces of student theatre" to be performed in Durham in 2013, and she has since turned it into an equally well-received short film. She hopes that her brave decision to turn her life story into a 'daringly honest record" will mean other sufferers of OCD can relate to her, as she understands the isolation the illness can cause. Hannah is honored to be part of such an esteemed project, can only hope the American audience will forgive her English spelling, and hopes the reader will gain something from such a diverse body of writers.

CHAPTER 24

I Am Recovering

By Hannah Brennan

At twenty, you're not supposed to be releasing anything autobiographical yet, because so far you've only had a brief sneeze of time with which to do something interesting. At twenty, putting the last year of my life on a stage was one of the hardest and yet most rewarding experiences I have had in my own little chunk of time so far.

In that story, I reduced my mental illness to three words:

Misunderstanding. Isolation. Tiredness.

Obsessive Compulsive Disorder as an illness is the victim of an ignorant media machine. "Obsessive Cleaners versus Compulsive Hoarders" does nothing to raise awareness, it just regresses potentially sympathetic people to views as one-dimensional as the programs themselves. In fact, when people learned I had OCD, I'd quite often catch them glancing at the splattering of ink on my hands, the clothes strewn across the bedroom floor, the tottering piles of books balancing on the very edges of surfaces, and the crumpled, unwashed haven of duvets that was my bed. I'd stare defiantly back, waiting for someone to comment on how ironic it was that I was messy.

And tick number one for misunderstanding.

In fact, to further illustrate this, I should probably mention Tom here. My best friend by chance: we shared a mental illness and a love of anything alcoholic. Tom has what one would term "contamination"

OCD. Toilets, washing up, bins, and laundry were daily minefields—and he couldn't afford to go wrong because hand-washing took up a good ten to fifteen minutes. Yet, when Tom walked into my mess of a room, he'd drop his coat on the floor, kick his shoes off, empty the wrappers and miscellaneous debris of the day onto the floor, and mosey on over for a chat. His own room never quite lived up to mine in mess terms, but the only area he kept organized was the whisky shelf.

People would also try and convince us that they too had OCD, and we'd blink politely at their plight: my ruler has to be perpendicular to my notebook when I'm in lectures—I'm such a freak! It's a bit heavy to claim you have a "real" mental illness, like depression, but OCD is a whimsical, slightly fashionable version you can prove you have by loudly exclaiming at the presence of mushrooms on your shelf in the fridge.

Tick the second for misunderstanding.

For me, misunderstanding went much deeper, however. Firstly, there was the fact that my OCD was manifesting itself in eating—meaning I had to deal daily with questions about my "anorexia." In fact, only being able to eat potatoes without having a panic attack was meaning I was developing what Tom would refer to as a "bit of chub"—and an adorable one at that.

My last example of misunderstanding is bound up with isolation: my own misunderstanding. I was terrified, because all of a sudden the brain that produced the exam results that landed me at a fantastic university? It was firing blanks. The only thing it could concentrate on was making me feel anxious and wound up.

I'd skip meals, binge on junk food, hoard the wrappers from things I'd eaten, record everything in a food diary, eat only with a fork and nothing else, give my food away, and yet I was determined that I couldn't have a mental illness. I'd grown up knowing depression was a part of our family's history, but anxiety was an altogether alien concept. There's an apt phrase from *The Bell Jar* I could use here:

"But I wasn't driving anything. Not even myself."

I AM!

Like a lot of teenage girls, *The Bell Jar* spoke to me across the Atlantic and across the fifty or so years, curled up in my bedroom in a South East suburb of London. Like Esther, I had fantastic prospects, and yet all I was capable of was torturing myself. My way out? I told myself I was attention-seeking. I didn't really have any discernable mental health issues, I was just determined to get attention somewhere, and I'd fake the most dramatic thing I could think of to get it.

Disgusted with the human being that could do such a thing, I started shutting people out.

Big fat tick for isolation.

What was really rough was the tiredness. I can sum this up best only by quoting myself. After almost six months of a steep downward spiral, I got help, and eighteen months later, I was well on the road to recovery. I decided to take a leap of faith and write my experiences down, and I was blessed to have them performed. The play was called *Soap and Water* to epitomize what Tom went through. He was not as lucky as I was—his OCD was onset from about eleven, possibly earlier, rather than eighteen, like mine. I felt like I'd made a difference, and I'd actively taken a step toward helping other people and coming to terms what I'd been through.

Back to tiredness, this is a scene from the play:

> F: I don't want it. I don't want this illness. I don't want it.
> M: I can't take it away.
> F: You have to. I'm so tired. I want a break, just one day where I cannot think about it, where I can get up and not eat and not get hungry and not have rules. I want to be normal. I want to worry about whether the sauce is burning, not whether the spoon for the sauce is the same spoon that I used for sweetcorn and not sauce two days ago. I'm so tired. I can't do it, I can't. I can't get up tomorrow morning unless you take this away. Give it to someone else.
> M: I can't.
> F: Give it to anyone. I don't deserve it. I haven't done anything wrong. I am so, so tired. I just want a break, just one day, please, give me just one day.

Although I cannot guarantee that is exactly how the conversation between me and Tom went, I think it sums it up pretty well. Producing all the adrenaline to keep that anxiety pumping is exhausting, and the state of being constantly on edge shreds your nerves. If I could have had a few days off to recuperate and sleep properly and rest, I'm confident I could have turned it around for me and Tom a lot quicker than I did. It's the physical impact of being so overwhelmed all the time.

It's a very long story, quite tragic in parts. I'd often thought it'd make a very good movie. Boy—long-term sufferer in an abusive relationship meets Girl—newly out of control. Boy shows Girl what it means to have and live with OCD. Girl and Boy go out and get wasted and Girl shouts or Boy cries. Boy slowly helps girl turn her illness around. Girl recovers, gives Boy the courage to end aforementioned abusive relationship. Girl and Boy continue to recover, become healthy and happy, and one day kiss in a nightclub while receiving a wet-willy from a stranger.

Modern romance at its finest. What this blockbuster-movie-fantasy made me realize, however, was that there was a way to record our experiences that would allow for longevity and an international audience. *Soap and Water* was remodeled into a short film, and we've since released it on YouTube and received some outstanding feedback.

Not everyone has an obligation to share their story to try and help other people. It was by pure coincidence that I, Hannah Brennan, aspiring playwright, was to develop OCD whilst at university, with opportunities for writing and performing so abundant. For me, my struggles with food are on such a minute scale they do not really register anymore, which is wonderful. For a while, I wanted to pretend it wasn't me who went doo-lally, as I affectionately put it. That worked about as well as one could have hoped: it didn't.

For me, making the film was a chance to accept what I had been through, and if it could challenge someone's misunderstanding of OCD, make someone feel less isolated, or give someone else a scrap of energy with which to start the fight, well then, I'd done something worthwhile.

OCD is more than just an acronym.

I AM!

For me and Tom? OCD was the mutual friend who introduced us, watched us fall in love, got insanely jealous, and left us to it.

Please take the time to watch our short film—the piece explores our story in more detail, and is a frank, honest, and un-dramatized version of events. By watching, sharing, and getting in touch with us, you can help use our story, and even yours, to teach people what it means to have Obsessive Compulsive Disorder, an anxiety disorder, or any other form of mental illness.

www.youtube.com/soapandwater2014

www.facebook.com/soapandwater2014

Amy Noiboonsook

I am blessed to be a stay-at-home mom. I am a very happily married mother of four boys. Joseph is sixteen, Samuel is fifteen, Christopher is ten, and Matthew is eight. I have been married to my luv for nineteen years and I'm looking forward to another fifty! I recently became an independent consultant for Scentsy (one of the best decisions of my life). I love that it had given me back my identity. I volunteer at both schools and try to make a difference in my kids' lives, as well all (450) kids at the elementary school.

CHAPTER 25

I Am Rare

By Amy Noiboonsook

The definition of unique: being the only one of its kind; unlike anything else. It took me a while to embrace this concept. As a young girl, I remember wanting so badly to be like everyone else. My parents made sure we had everything—the shoes, clothes, toys that all the kids had. I guess as a kid you think you need those "cool" things that help you fit in. I, of course, didn't realize no matter what you have, you are not going to be happy until you are content with yourself.

If I could speak to my teenage self, I would say that everything will work out exactly how it should. I know it was hard to see then, but all the hurtful comments and bullying will make you stronger. I didn't want to be stronger, I wanted to be liked. Don't get me wrong, I had a couple of girls that were my true friends and one that I consider my sister. But it's those girls that made fun of my hair and skin color that really drove me to try to be nicer.

If you were wondering my ethnic background is one that is unique. My mother is Mexican and Chinese and my father is from Thailand. Quite a mix, don't you think? I love to have so much culture in my family, and I realize now that I'm lucky to have grown up with such a diverse family. I grew up eating tortillas, rice, and beans at my abuelita's house, and then the next weekend it was rice, Bok Choy, and coconut chicken at my grandmother's house.

One instance I remember vividly is when a Hispanic girl had pointed out in front of all the girls in the locker room that I was "trying to look like a chola." She made fun of my hair and makeup. I think what hurt me most was when she said "why are you trying to be Mexican?" I wanted to shout out, "I am Mexican!" But of course, being the shy person I was, I didn't want to make anyone mad to talk back. How could she not know that I was part Mexican? I grew up in Boyle Heights, which is predominantly Hispanic. I speak Spanish and cook Mexican dishes! What more proof did she want? As much as I tried to get away from all the negative, I just couldn't. When we moved back to Walnut, I enrolled my son in the elementary school and who do I see? Yes, it was the girl that tormented me in middle school! She doesn't have any power over me now, right? Wrong. As soon I saw her, I reverted to being an awkward preteen. In that moment, I realized how much a couple of words can haunt a person. I stepped out of my comfort zone and said hello. She said hello and nothing else. Did she not remember what she did and how mean she was? I should have said that she hurt my feelings and she shattered my self-confidence. But I didn't. To this day, every time I see her, I cringe. It makes me nervous to have her son in the same class as mine. What if he tries to bully my son? How can I protect him without being an overprotective mom? I figure all I can do is let the values I instilled in him take over and hope for the best.

As a parent now of four boys—Joseph, Samuel, Christopher and Matthew—I instill in them that it's OK to be different. It's actually a privilege to have such a colorful family. I have them ask my dad about his childhood and his experiences. My mom loves to share her grade school memories, as well. My parents are hardworking and very supportive. That is what I want my boys to remember, not all the negative things kids say and do to pull you down.

My youngest, Matt, has already experienced some of this bullying. He is the one that is most like me. He wants everyone to be his friend and can't understand why when it doesn't happen. It breaks my heart that kids say things without realizing the consequences. I know it's learned and it's not really their fault, but it hurts never the less. This is what compels me to volunteer at the schools. I am trying to leave them with happy, positive memories and hopefully along the way, spread the message of being tolerant. I do see the fruit of my labor when the kids say, "Hi, Teacher," or, "She works at the school," when I see them at the grocery store. That makes everything I do worth all the long days and running around.

My oldest son, Joe, is finally coming into his own and embracing a culture that is not really ours. He has found a club on campus that he has some interest in and has dived in headfirst. He is in Polynesian Club and just performed the Haka in front of the whole school! I love it! That was a proud mom moment. I think the Island culture appealed to him because they are an accepting people. I know I am doing something right when I see them do these things on their own.

Sam, my second born, just has that calming and loving spirit. He is comfortable in his own skin and just accepts everyone for who they are. I am kind of jealous of how quickly he has mastered this and that it took me so long to get to this point. I know he will achieve great things and that he doesn't have to suffer through all that I did.

Chris is my middle child and has this presence that I'm so impressed by. He is my intellectual one and will analyze everything. I think that's why he has not been affected by all of the nonsense. He loves with his whole heart, and it doesn't crumble when it's not reciprocated.

I am so blessed to have such an amazing husband that loves me for who I am and embraces my unique mixture. I met Norbert over nineteen years ago and he says the thing attracted him to me is my skin color and my exotic look. What?! I can't believe after all the years someone could look at me and love me for who I was! I hit the lotto! He is supportive, loving, and my best friend. His family was a little shocked when they first met me. I was the first Asian that was introduced to the family. To their surprise, I speak Spanish and know the culture, so I fit right in. It took a while for everyone to be comfortable enough to speak Spanish with me—they just assumed that I only spoke English. It's kind of fun to see their reaction when I respond to what they are saying in Spanish.

I realize now how lucky I am to have such a unique background. I now look forward to people I meet asking what I am. I Am Rare!

Craig J. Boykin

Craig J. Boykin is a renowned speaker and author. Craig has devoted his life to creating lasting change for those who desire it. Craig has risen to the national stage by delivering his inspirational message, which tells people how to shake off mediocrity and live up to their greatness. Craig published a book in 2013 entitled, *My Life, Your Inspiration,* and has also been featured on TBN. Craig is one of the most sought after speakers in America. In February of 2014, Craig spoke at the Department of Justice in Washington, DC, as the keynote speaker for Black History Month.

CHAPTER 26

I Am Understanding

By Craig J. Boykin

I understand…

I understand that from birth, it seems as if the odds were stacked against you. I understand that your mother's actions may not be typical of a loving mother. I understand that the pain you feel because of the lack of love and affection shown by her has left you with a great void. I understand that your father may not have been involved in your life. I understand that it is as if the educational system and teachers don't understand you, nor do they understand that your situation and circumstances at home affects your learning, daily. I understand that in some cases, the educational system will place in you special education for behavioral problems because they are baffled on how to reach you.

I understand the pressures you are challenged with in the streets and neighborhoods across America. I understand that any sign of mental and physical weakness will get you killed quickly. Therefore, I understand the need to give off the attitude of "**I DON'T CARE**" to protect yourself. I understand that you have been hurt countless times by others and now you have closed up.

I understand that education isn't important to you because very few in your family are benefiting from an education, so you don't understand the benefit of having one. I understand that after working countless low-paying jobs, the attraction of doing something illegal becomes very attractive, for the simple fact that you still have a family to feed and bills to pay. I understand that it can become very frustrating, living pay check to pay check and in poverty.

I understand that the instantaneous gratification of selling drugs, robbing, and stealing are real because you feel that this is a means to an end for your situation. I understand that in your eyes, prison is just eventually something you will have to face because it's a part of the "game." I understand that if individuals stopped judging you because of your appearance and vocabulary, and actually sat down and spoke with you, they would see that you are more than your situation, and in most cases, you have to act the way you do to protect yourself from being hurt!

I understand that it seems as if you are always being profiled by individuals in the criminal justice system. I understand that you didn't understand the magnitude of your actions. I understand that now you have a felony and it seems as if life is over. I understand that your struggle in life is very real!

However…

What you need to understand is that the exact same way you figured out how to survive in the harsh conditions of your environment, allows you to have the same power to overcome that lifestyle, and it all starts with one decision.

What you need to understand is that I endured numerous hardships, which I now often credit for my passion for helping those who are less fortunate. My mother was a product of a broken home. She didn't have a relationship with her biological father. As a homeless high school dropout, physically and emotionally abused, she gave birth to me at age sixteen. My mother began drinking and using drugs almost daily. Her relationships with men throughout my childhood were very toxic. In elementary school, my grades began to fall. I began to act out and got suspended from school often. My teachers and counselors became very concerned with my actions and decided to have me "tested." I was ultimately diagnosed with a learning disability and placed in special education classes. Due to my difficulties in school, I repeated the third and fifth grade.

Consequently, by the time I was in the tenth grade, I was two years older than most of my classmates, and I still didn't hold the necessary skills to write a five-sentence paragraph. Overwhelmed, I ultimately dropped out of high school, thus continuing the cycle of high school dropouts in my family. My mother, father, brother, and sister all dropped out of high school. Confused about life, I began engaging in dangerous activities that led me to land in jail. I was also shot.

Having hit rock bottom, I realized that change was needed. I decided to enroll in the Job Corps career program, which allowed me to earn both my GED and a diploma in retail sales. Immediately upon graduating from Job Corps, I enlisted in the US army. It was in the military that I developed integrity and discipline.

Despite being encouraged to attend a community college, I enrolled in one of the most challenging four-year universities in my hometown. In spite of the educational challenges I faced with a GED, learning disability, and the pressures of failing, three years later, I graduated with a bachelor's degree in Business Administration from Auburn University Montgomery. I went on to earn a master's degree in Theology and a master's degree in Criminal Justice, both from Faulkner University. Understand that I AM currently working on my PhD in adult education.

I understand that you are powerful beyond measure and that you are more than ALL of the above. How do I know? Because I was once like you.

The first step in understanding is **CARPE DIEM**.

Carpe Diem is a phrase originating from the Latin language, meaning *seize the day*. This phrase has begun to be used to motivate people all over the world, to stop messing around, and to live life on the edge. What about you? Are you living your life to the fullest, or just simply existing? What are you missing out on while sitting on the sidelines? Life is too short to settle for merely existing. Don't miss out on all that life has to offer you. Learn to live in this moment! My challenge for each person reading these words is to go out and do something today that pushes you out of your comfort zone. Do something that really makes you feel alive!

The second step in understanding is the need to **Eliminate EXCUSES**

Understand that Bill Gates' first business failed, Albert Einstein didn't speak until he was four years old, Jim Carrey was homeless, Benjamin Franklin dropped out of school at age ten, Stephen King's first novel was rejected thirty times, Oprah Winfrey gave birth at age fourteen and lost her child, Thomas Edison failed one thousand times before creating the light bulb, Vincent Van Gogh only sold one painting in his lifetime. (Van Gogh is considered one of the greatest artists of all time, yet the poor guy only sold one painting the entire time he was alive), Simon Cowell had a failed record company, and Steven Spielberg was rejected from USC — twice!

Feed Your **DREAMS**

Whatever you feed grows, and whatever you starve dies.

Imagine you have a little ugly unwanted weed growing in your backyard, and next to it, you have a beautiful and fragrant rose. Whichever one you spend time cultivating will grow. And the one you don't cultivate will ultimately perish. This is my attempt at understanding how you can overcome "weeds" in your life. Whatever it is that trips you up and has a hold on you can be starved to death. Whatever your dreams in life are, you can grow them by feeding them, so start today.

WRITE YOUR OWN STORY

Life is like a game of poker — you are dealt a hand, and only you can decide what to keep and what to throw back…

In life, we are dealt a number of factors that are not of our choosing. We do not choose the genes we are born with. We do not choose to be male or female. We do not choose the characteristics of our parents and the way they treat us. Some of us are lucky enough to be dealt strong hands at the beginning of the game of life. We are born with genes that predispose us toward traits that increase our chance of success in life: intelligence, energy, a cheerful disposition, self- discipline, composure and resiliency, and creativity. Some of us are not so lucky. We are dealt hands that predispose us toward low intelligence, lethargy, antipathy, impulsiveness and attention deficits, irritability, and lack of imagination. Our parents fail to support us or actively abuse us. We live in underprivileged neighborhoods, where crime, drug use, and other dangers run rampant.

Life is like a game of poker—you are dealt a hand, and only you can decide what to keep and what to throw back...

MAKE LIFE COUN`T

THIS MOMENT IS YOURS!

I need you to understand that you, and you alone, must decide to act. This moment is your golden opportunity to break away from the limitations of the past, and to live and act with a positive resolve. You must stop worrying about what has happened in the past, the opportunities you have let slip by, or the hurt that others may have imposed on you, for there is nothing you can do now to undo what has already happened. But you do have the power, at this very moment, to change your life for the better. Any day we wish, we can discipline ourselves to change it all.

Kat Bickert aka Karunaji

Kat Bickert is a business savvy yogini and meditation instructor whose passion lies around helping others create more peace and bliss from within. Her yogi name means Mother of Compassion, and it is compassion that she uses as a tool to create deeper connections within ourselves and with the universe around us. It was yoga and meditation that saved her from the pain and turmoil of a traumatic accident, but the blissful spiritual experiences and understandings that came from her years of practice became the greatest gift that she could receive and ultimately share with the world. It is the path of yoga that allows her to share with others the path to each their own Cosmic Liberation.

CHAPTER 27

I Am Still

By Kat Bickert aka Karunaji

Be silent. Be still, and know thy true self. These words entered my mind in meditation and have become a mantra of mine. It is amazing to me to think that I meditate at all, let alone have tremendously fulfilling journeys and experiences in meditation. I have experienced highs like no drug can induce, simply by coming into myself and allowing the stillness to set in, as my true radiant self is revealed to me. In this stillness, I can witness the greatness of who I am.

It wasn't always this way. In fact, I was lost, alone, scattered, and subject to the changing winds of life that carried me away like a seed. Having no idea who I was or what I wanted, jaded by the separation of my parents, I spent my high school days worrying myself sick over what I was to do with the rest of my life. The first girl in a family of five boys, I was moved more by what others thought I should be, or what I would be good at, than by the quiet whisper of a voice within. The voice of which I had no idea how to hear. A sense of panic made me feel like life was speeding by me while I moved at an achingly slow snail's pace toward a solution to my suffering.

Crippled by my insecurities, my mind ran rampant, riddling me with judgment, guilt, and self-criticisms. Nothing I ever did was ever going to be good enough. No matter what I did, I would fail. I felt defeated and alone. At night, I would stay up preoccupying my mind with artwork and poetry, dreaming for everything to just stop. All I really wanted was for everything to just stop.

I didn't realize that this feeling was a message calling out to me to just sit with myself. Sounds simple enough, but let me tell you, it's not. Meditation is a simplistic practice, meaning that it has very little to it in terms of instructions; however, it is very challenging work. The brighter the light you shine into the unknown, the farther you can see into the darkness. However, unveiling the creatures that loom in the darkness of the mind can be very rewarding. We see how frail these monsters and demons truly are in comparison to the light inside of ourselves.

Think of it this way. You are standing in the middle of New York Times Square. This represents your mind. Each of the many cars that pass by represents your many thoughts. You are the witness to all of these thoughts. The beauty of the practice is that you can move yourself, you can change your focus, and you can become unattached to the thoughts that pass you by. This occurs through a devoted practice of meditation.

You aren't going to chase the cab you are hailing up the street four blocks to see where it's going, or make it stop for you. You stay still. Another will come soon enough. Your thoughts are always moving. The noise of these thoughts is amplified by the closed-in walls of the high rises, and the horizon can't be seen clearly in this space. This is the state of overwhelm and confusion. You begin to feel boxed in. Imprisoned.

The aim of the game is to find a place where no thoughts come to be. A place of silence. A place of stillness. A place of serenity. Sometimes it is our thoughts that begin to move us. But when we stay in our thoughts, we can never become still. We cannot experience ourselves truly when we are in our thoughts. We become distracted and motion sick.

We can allow our thoughts to take us out of the city, to a place where there are no buildings to trap in the bustling sounds of the many thoughts. But the key to a deeper meditation is to get out of your thoughts. Eventually, you will have to get out of the "car" in order for the experience of true meditation to begin.

Imagine getting out of your thoughts and coming to a calmer more beautiful place. Picture a field with mountains on the horizon and a beautiful sunset. Your thoughts have brought you here. This can't be all bad, can it? But it's not the beautiful imagery within your mind that creates the bliss of deep meditation. This field is a gateway. Walking into the field, away from the roadway where our thoughts pass us by, we can find a place to sit, on our own, in nature.

Lie down in the field and look at the heavens. Out here, away from your thoughts, you become a witness to nature. You can become an observer, and you can eventually enter the witness state. When you master this state of being—to witness—the circumstances of your life hold no power over you. You greet each situation with compassion and understanding. You stand before it with presence and awareness, rather than being carried away by the thoughts that drive you crazy, back and forth, from the past to the future.

So here you are, at first carried by the thoughts to a new place in the mind. Carried to a place in the mind where the thoughts disappear. Now, we use the mind, to go beyond the mind. As the sun sets in the setting of our mind, the stars come out and we are surrounded by darkness. In this darkness, light shines through.

Now, the stars are a metaphor for the stars themselves. The Cosmos. The universe. Energy in all its vast and infinite forms. The beauty of meditation happens when we forget the mind. We forget that we have a body, and that we are in a field on the earth, looking into the stars. When we forget the mind, we become one with the stars. We merge with the Cosmos.

A deep resonating vibration penetrates our being as we sit and witness ourselves as a totally expanded form of energy—with no body, no mind, no breath, and no need to guide the experience. No choice. We experience choicelessness. This only happens when we surrender to nature and let go of the mind.

Now, hearing all this and experiencing it are two completely different things. Had I known about meditation and how greatly it would change my life, I would have begun when I was five years of age. I think of all the great challenges I've faced in my life and that what made them so upsetting was that they threw me off balance so easily. I was so easily moved by what was happening around me.

But I've come to know that no matter how great the storm in our lives, when we are still within, we become unmovable. We are given an opportunity to remove ourselves from our circumstances, to look at the situation objectively from outside of the chaos of the storm, without attachment. We create a safe haven for ourselves where we can step back and take a look at the big picture, to see all the connections. Rather than being carried away by our thoughts and our troubles, we can step into a place where we have space to breathe. We come to a place where all is calm and quiet. A place where we need only to ask the right questions, and the answers are revealed to us in the most profound of ways.

And asking the right question is indeed a very important piece of this puzzle. We cannot continue to ask the questions that lead us back into the storm—like, "Why is this happening to me?" or, "Why couldn't it have been different?" All of my experience has taught me that we must come to a place of acceptance—of all the good, the bad, and the atrocious—in order to move through it. There is no moving around it. When we move through our sufferings with acceptance, and by embracing them, we are able to become free of them, and even empowered by them. We become greater for having been through them and coming out the other side.

So then we come back into inside, to the stillness of "I am," and meditate. We meditate on whatever we like. Set an intention, or say a prayer, and begin. We ask a question that leads us to the solution. "How can I overcome this depression?" "How can I be free from my circumstances?" "What must I do in order to be happy?" Then you sit, become still, and listen. When a thought comes up, take note and let go. Come back to the stillness within and listen to the silence.

Listen to the voice within you. Listen to the great knowledge that fills you. I can tell you that I would have never believed myself to be wise or knowledgeable. But after experiencing the depths of myself, I realize that we all have the capacity for great knowledge, strength, and compassion. We need only to get to know ourselves more deeply. When we can see ourselves in a deeper and more pure light of our true essence within, self-doubt, fear, anxiety, self-judgment are all absolved. The truth is more powerful and real. The illusions of our powerlessness are revealed as lies.

I AM!

I know that right now this can be a little hard to believe or trust. But all I'm asking is for you to get to know yourself, as I did. I've been through the wringer. It seemed at many points that sadness and chaos would be all I knew. I would look at the world in anger and hate for the terrible things we've all been doing to each other. But we can only experience peace when each of us discovers how to experience peace from within. For me, I have experienced peace by coming to know the stillness within me.

I am still.

You are too. You may just have not felt it yet. But with practice, you will. I know it.

Roosevelt "DJ" Standifer, Jr.

Roosevelt is a seasoned business and community organizer in the South Georgia/North Florida region. He has extensive experience in Financial Planning and Marketing as an advisor with Waddell & Reed, Inc. of Atlanta, as well as international team building, project management, and marketing for national non-profit organizations and Christian ministries. Roosevelt is Senior Consultant managing Strategic Partnerships for Strategy Group. Roosevelt holds BA in Business Administration from Valdosta State University.

CHAPTER 28

1 Am Bridging

By Roosevelt "DJ" Standifer, Jr

Over the years, I have learned that many gifts as a child that I possess could have created more fruit in my life if I were more aware of its potential. Just imagine, if you asked anyone the question, "Would you like to be more successful in your life?" I do not know many people that would answer, "No..." And if they did say no, you might want to make sure that they are not driving home because they just might be drunk. I am almost sure that everyone would like to see more fruit in their life. To the person that answers yes to this question, it simply means that you need to cross over a bridge from the land of unfruitfulness to fruitfulness. You might say, I am not unfruitful but just not as fruitful as I would like to be. Well, it takes a bridge to help a person to crossover a stream, a river, or in some cases a sea of unfruitfulness. The eighteenth chapter of Proverbs and the sixteenth verse in the Bible gives us a key understanding about how our gifts can bring us into opportunities because who we come into contact with. A man's gift maketh room for him, and bringeth him before great men... Well, as you become wiser in life, you'll come to the realization that a bridge is a wonderful gift for anyone who is in need to cross over something that's difficult. I found that a bridge becomes a blessing to you when it supports you to get through a messy situation and create more fruit in your life.

I was born in that late 70s in a town on the outskirts of Atlanta, Georgia, called Kennesaw. This town is probably best known for its gun law that requires everyone to own their own firearm The rationale was that it was supposed to protect the citizens of the town from the various groups, like the Ku Klux Klan. To understand a bit of the history of the town, let me paint the picture here of how I grew up. My family was the only black family in our neighborhood, which meant I was the only black kid on the bus ride to school every morning. In a school that had only a very few different ethnic groups, kids, needless to say, are very mean and say the most hurtful things to people just because of the difference between the color of someone's skin. That was the most difficult thing to overcome when growing up for me. My grandmother taught all of our family that no matter what a person might say or do, you should always look up and smile. My grandmother's words became a bridge for me many times in life, to help me overcome different situations when the other kids would make remarks and derogatory comments about me because I was a different color. Although the remarks were hurtful, I realized that they would only say what they heard a parent or someone else say before in front of them. I have always wanted to believe the best is in everyone—it's just hard sometimes to pull it out of them. I learned that laughter and the ability to make friends would help me during difficult times, when people would say things that were not always so pleasant. I embraced it to help me see other peoples' lives change, even when they would say some of the most hurtful things. At school one day, I was walking in the cafeteria where I witnessed this one girl, who looked as mean as a snake, say," N****r, get out of my way, you are standing to close to me." I looked the girl who made this terrible comment directly in her eyes without a word for a few seconds, while she looked at me back with a straight face. I smiled and just gently laughed and walked away from her. Later in life, this same girl would become a close friend during our school years. She also told me later that what made her hate black people so much. All those years before meeting me, her parents told her a story at a young age that made her cross a bridge in her mind to treat some people a certain way based on the color of their skin. Her parents became a bridge for her to cross over to a certain place where it was OK to treat and say things to certain types of people. Later in life, when I became her bridge, she realized that the place that her parents helped her to cross over to was wrong. A bridge can take you somewhere you've never been before, it can take you somewhere bad or take you some place good. This is why it is extremely important to always be aware of the bridges you cross.

A bridge does not only have to be just a place or thing—a bridge can also be a person, too, and can lead people across to a good place or take them across to bad places, sometimes. How do you know if you are leading someone to a good place, you might ask? Well, when he or she accepts the very life of God living through their body, to do the heavenly Father's business, you will desire to lead people to a better place. A life lived for God allows you to become like the brick and mortar of a strong built bridge. Your life then becomes an instrument that will allow people to walk across so that they may reach the other side to a better place. You become a support system, and when this gift of being a bridge is activated in you, it simply becomes more natural, for the effort it takes to help others. This gift allows things to be connected rather than pulled apart. It's not only to help people with their problems—sometimes it is helping them cross into a refreshing new life change, or giving them fresh ideas, so that life can become shared. For the individual who possesses the gift of being a bridge when fully aware of its power and potential, anything is possible.

All good gifts come from above! So it is very important to denote the origin and source of any gift that is given. When we take ownership over anything, we also then must become responsible for maintaining whatever it is that we claim to own. House, car, or wife—just a joke, my wife would never in a millions years go for that nonsense. I own nothing. However, God has entrusted me with much. When a gift never becomes an idol, our natural ability to operate in that gift becomes more graceful. As an example, the Bible allows us to gain another key understanding in the book of Luke. In the fifth chapter, people were working and doing business as usual. However, we learn about a fisherman whose business was not doing well at all. In fact, his business was very unfruitful, causing the man to work later than normal. But once this fisherman was taught by the Master, he went back to work in the business market and was obedient to follow the Master's instruction. He tapped into a new source that came from obedience to what a person taught him. The Master was a bridge for the fisherman. The Master was also Christ; needless to say, the result of that fisherman was undeniable…he went across a bridge that forever changed his life. After he crossed that bridge, it turned his unsuccessful business into a thriving business—more fruit in his life.

A bridge can look very different based upon the need of each individual and past experience. However, never allow your judgment stop you from being taught by others that are willing to support you and become a bridge to you. Sometimes, we just need to be still to know that God has a plan to bring you out of whatever you might be going through that is causing you conflict or pain. Look for your bridge to cross. Be a bridge, because you are a bridge. Just always remember that the gift of being a bridge is not always fun or exciting. It sometimes is very challenging and hurtful, and that is why you must never forget that it is God's life living in you. God is the source of our strength and we are merely vessels for his honor. We can clearly identify people in our lives that have been the structures that have carried us over many obstacles. People that have helped us to get onto the solid ground by sticking with us to overcome bad experiences, or even bad habits. Thank them. They became bridges to help us at just the right time and season of our life.

You are not alone! Don't let that something become greater in your life than it needs to be. It does not have power over you; it only has the power that you give it. A bridge will help you walk over that situation or any circumstance that might have brought you down or created your depression. Find your bridge and go across. Become a bridge for someone else and teach them all that you have been taught!

Conclusion

I trust that if you made it this far, you have been able to realize that you are not alone. Although you may be experiencing undeniable pain and valid feelings, you can now embrace the opportunity for change. Through honest self-reflection, positivity, courage, hope, and faith, you can move forward into a better life. You can allow yourself a life that is not defined by your past pain or experiences.

As I read through these chapters myself, I was able to identify with each of the co-authors. With each intimate encounter, I was filled with a vast array of emotion. I could empathize with and feel each soul as my body was overcome with glory bumps. Did you have a similar experience? Although our life journeys have been our own, there are more similarities than there are differences. Who did you relate most to?

I am sure that there was no mistake in you coming across this compilation. There is a plan that is so much greater than what we can even comprehend, and it works for our greater good. We have a purpose here in this life, and once we allow ourselves to grow past the barriers that are constructed to hold us back, we will be able to fulfill the plan that was uniquely designed for each of us. I pray that you will continue to define areas in your life, which need a little more positive self-talk—because your positive words, your self-love, and encouraging belief in yourself have the power to transform your life.

"Transformation"
A poem by: Judith LeBlanc

The caterpillar crawls and eats
Never in repose
Day and night her appetite
Grows, and grows, and grows.
It makes one shudder to watch her
Devouring everything in her way
Her ugliness, her greediness

Keeping everyone away.
Then one day when the sun goes down
Hiding its face behind a cloud
Without understanding she begins to spin
And she weaves her own funeral shroud.
One day while walking in the woods
In the cool of a late afternoon
I glanced up and caught a glimpse
Of an old and withered cocoon.
I considered the seemingly futile life
Of the worm who lay buried within
To have been so hated and reviled
For her ugliness, greed, and sin.
Suddenly I noticed movement
Within the cocoon upon the branch
It twitched and stretched and moved about
Like some strange and eerie dance.
Oh, silly worm! Why struggle so hard
To return to this cold, cruel life?
All it ever had to offer to you
Were hatred, grief and strife.
I watched with a sense of wonder
As the creature began to dig
A hole at the end of the shriveled cocoon
Then she climbed out onto a twig.
A cool breeze blew across her wet back
Her body slowly began to dry
I watched with awe as she unfurled wings
Like gossamer jewels against the sky.
I observed with great joy as she fluttered
Her lacy wings upon the air
Then suddenly, quietly, she flew away
Her death shroud remaining there.
That day I learned a great lesson
That the worm within must die
And go to the grave, and wither away
To release the butterfly.

I AM!

AMY NOIBOONSOOK · ANGIE TOPBAS · ANTHONY J. SOAVE

ASHLEY LOVE · BERNARD J. RABINE · PASTOR TIM MCCONNELL

BRIEANNA P. DAUGHERTY · CHRIS MUSGROVE · CRAIG J. BOYKIN

EMILY OBUKOWICZ · EVELYN "THE HEART LADY" POLK · HANNAH BRENNAN

JUDITH LEBLANC · KAT BICKERT AKA KARUNAJI · KIMLE NAILER

COMPILED BY **NICOLE EASTMAN**, D.O.

MARISA ANNE CLAIRE

NICOLE EASTMAN

PARA-CHAPLAIN MICHELLE SMITH

ROOSEVELT "DJ" STANDIFER, JR

SAMANTHA SMITH

SHANNON MONTICCIOLO-DAVIS

SHEILAH M. WILSON

SUNITI SAXENA

SUZANNE M. GABLI

TIM EASTMAN

TYESHA K. LOVE

VICKI SAVINI

WARREN BROAD

The End

CPSIA information can be obtained at www.ICGtesting.com
Printed in the USA
BVOW01s2327080514

352917BV00003B/8/P